A guide to
Marx's *Capital*

D0840915

A guide to Marx's *Capital*

ANTHONY BREWER

Department of Economics,
University of Bristol

CAMBRIDGE UNIVERSITY PRESS

Cambridge
London   New York   New Rochelle
Melbourne   Sydney

Published by the Press Syndicate of the University of Cambridge
The Pitt Building, Trumpington Street, Cambridge CB2 1RP
32 East 57th Street, New York, NY 10022, USA
296 Beaconsfield Parade, Middle Park, Melbourne 3206, Australia

First published 1984

Printed in Great Britain at the University Press, Cambridge

Library of Congress catalogue card number: 83-14329

British Library Cataloguing in Publication Data

Brewer, Anthony
A guide to Marx's Capital.
1. Marx, Karl. Das Kapital
I. Title
335.4   HB501.M37

ISBN 0 521 25730 1 hard covers
ISBN 0 521 27626 4 paperback

WD

TO JANET

Contents

VOLUME 3. THE PROCESS OF CAPITALIST PRODUCTION AS A WHOLE

Preface

Marx's *Capital* is one of the most important and influential books ever written. Anyone who wants to understand the modern world should read it. Unfortunately it is a rather offputting book. Some of the difficulties of reading it are inevitable, since unfamiliar and complex ideas are never easy to grasp, but it seems more forbidding than it really is. Marx's terminology and style of argument may seem strange at first, and the first few chapters are the most abstract and difficult, but the reader who persists will find it worth the effort.

My aim in this guide is to make *Capital* more accessible. The main body of the guide is a chapter by chapter commentary on *Capital*, identifying and explaining the main threads of Marx's argument. I have picked out particular passages for special comment when they mark a critical step in the analysis or when they deal with large issues which Marx did not write about at length elsewhere.

To do this, of course, means making judgements about what is important, and about what Marx meant, but I have tried to stick as close to the text as I can, and to leave it to the reader to draw conclusions. I have deliberately avoided detailed discussion of debates over the interpretation of Marx's theory, since this is a guide to *Capital*, not to Marxism in general. I have provided some references to debates on specific issues, as a starting point for further reading, but I have made no attempt to be comprehensive. A full guide to the immense body of secondary literature would fill another book.

Capital is available in many different editions with different page numbers, and even different chapter, part and volume numbers (some versions of volume one are divided into two 'volumes'). The chapter titles used in this guide (and listed in the table of contents) should be sufficient to allow readers to identify the corresponding chapters in other editions. I have used the Moscow edition, which is probably more widely available than any other (it is published under various imprints in different countries). I give all cross-references by volume, part, chapter and section, rather than by page numbers, so that they can be found in any edition. In terminology, I have followed the Aveling and Moore translation of volume one (as does the Moscow edition), since it was approved by Engels. One choice may be controversial; I have followed the standard translations in referring to persons of unspecified gender in the masculine (he, his, etc.) since it would have been cumbersome and artificial to do otherwise.

The introduction is intended to set *Capital* in the context of Marx's life and of his work as a whole. It also introduces some of the other writers to whom Marx frequently referred. Appendix one is a brief discussion of some of the forewords and afterwords by Marx and Engels to different editions and volumes of *Capital*. Appendix two deals with the *Communist Manifesto* and appendix three with the preface and introduction to *A Contribution to the Critique of Political Economy*. These short works complement *Capital*. Finally, I provide a glossary of Marx's technical terms.

I would like to thank Janet Brewer and Paul Bowles for helpful comments, and Marjorie Lunt for her skill and patience in typing the manuscript. They cannot be blamed for any remaining errors.

Introduction

The material facts of Marx's life can be summarized quite briefly. He was born in 1818, in the Rhineland, which had been incorporated into the growing Prussian empire a few years earlier. In 1836 he went to the University of Berlin, and in 1841 he obtained a doctorate with a dissertation on ancient philosophy. In the following two years he edited two radical journals, first the *Rheinische Zeitung* in the Rhineland, and then the *Deutsche-Französische Jahrbücher*, published in Paris but aimed at a German readership. Both fell foul of the Prussian authorities, and Marx retreated to Brussels as an exile. In the revolutionary year of 1848, he was able to return to Germany and edit another journal, the *Neue Rheinische Zeitung*, but was again driven into exile, this time in London.

The rest of his life, from 1849 to 1883, was spent as an exile in England. He never again held a regular job, and had to get by on legacies, gifts and occasional earnings from free-lance journalism. For much of this time he was poor and dogged by ill health. Until the last few years of his life, his political impact was negligible.

If the life of this obscure exile is of interest today, it is entirely because of the ideas that he produced.

Up to the mid-1840s, Marx's views were being formed, and were changing very rapidly as he absorbed ideas from a number of sources. In 1843–4, he became a socialist, started a lifelong collaboration and friendship with Friedrich Engels, and took up the study of economics.

In 1845, working with Engels, he arrived at a new system of thought, 'historical materialism', which he held to for the remainder of his life. Society, he argued, evolves through a succession of

1

stages, each with a distinctive economic structure. The latest stage, capitalism, was to be overthrown by a revolution led by the working class. His overarching theory of history and his immediate political programme were linked by an analysis of capitalism in which economic development generates both increasingly severe economic crises and sharpening class polarization, thus setting the stage for the coming revolution.

To begin with, the analysis was only sketched out. When he was forced into exile after 1848, Marx settled down to provide a more complete account. *Capital* was the final result.

1. From Hegel to historical materialism

Hegel

Intellectual life in Germany, when Marx was a student, was dominated by the philosophy of Hegel. Marx first resisted, then became an ardent Hegelian. Although he later rejected many of Hegel's ideas, his whole way of thinking was very fundamentally shaped by them.

According to Hegel, history is not a random sequence of events, but a comprehensible process, governed by objective laws which can only be grasped by looking at history as a whole. It is not, however, a story of uniform progress in a single direction, but a 'dialectical' process. Each stage of development is characterized by 'contradictions' between opposing forces, which are reconciled in a higher synthesis in the next stage, only to generate new contradictions. In broad terms Marx held to this view of history all of his life. When he broke with Hegel, it was Hegel's 'idealism' that he rejected. Idealism, in the technical, philosophical sense, is the view that 'mind' or 'ideas' are primary, and physical matter secondary. According to Hegel, history is primarily the story of the development of 'reason' or 'spirit'. Each period and each country has its own distinctive set of ideas, and the dialectical development of ideas is the motor of history.

Hegel's writings are extremely obscure, and can be interpreted in many ways. German philosophy in the 1830s and 1840s was riven by disputes between different schools of Hegelians. Hegel himself was dead, and was therefore unable to join in. The conservative version presented the Prussian state as the highest embodiment of reason, the culmination of history. This somewhat parochial view was understandably popular with officialdom.

Marx associated for a time with the opposing school of 'young Hegelians', who stressed instead the dynamic elements in Hegel, the emphasis on continual change, and who directed their iconoclasm particularly against established religion. Their style was, in Isaiah Berlin's words, 'an extraordinary compound of pedantry and arrogance, full of obscure paradoxes and laboured epigrams, embedded in alliterative, punning prose' (*Karl Marx*, 4th edn (Oxford University Press, 1978), p. 53). Marx's early works were written in this style, and are very tedious to read. He never quite shook off its influence, as can be seen in some passages in *Capital*.

Socialism

Marx was also influenced, in the early 1840s, by socialist writings. The terms 'socialist' and 'communist' had no very clear meaning at the time. Today, 'socialism' means, above all, opposition to 'capitalism', and the concept of capitalism as a distinct form of society did not exist until Marx invented it. Socialist writers in Marx's time rejected existing society on moral grounds, and presented blueprints of a better society to replace it. Some of their proposals were undeniably cranky, though that was not the main point of Marx's criticism.

Marx rejected existing socialist theories as 'utopian'. He insisted that history is governed by objective laws, which cannot be changed simply by saying that things ought to be different, any more than water can be made to run uphill by telling it that it ought to do so. Although he certainly detested capitalism, he regarded moral outrage as irrelevant, and aimed instead to show that a socialist revolution was a logical and necessary outcome of capitalist development. The organization of a future society would be determined by its people as they went along, and could not be forecast in detail.

Another major strand in Marx's thinking came from political economy (as economics was then called). The development of Marx's economics will be discussed in more detail below. It is enough to note here that he was still a beginner in economics in 1844–5, and took most of his technical economic analysis from other writers. The essential idea that he found in the literature was the concept of an economy as a coherent system governed by objective laws. In the new view that he was constructing, the process of economic development replaced Hegel's 'spirit' or 'reason' as the motor of history.

Historical materialism

All of these influences coalesced into a new theoretical framework during the years 1844 and 1845. Marx and Engels were working very closely together at the time, and must share the credit for the new system. The fact that they drew on ideas from a variety of sources in no way diminishes the importance or originality of their achievement; all great thinkers build on the work of their predecessors.

Marx had already arrived at one central idea when he wrote a set of notes or rough drafts in 1844 (known as the *Economic and Philosophical Manuscripts* or *Paris Manuscripts*). Here he focussed for the first time on what was to become the main theme of *Capital*, the relation between capital and wage-labour, capitalist and worker. The capitalist owns the means of production (equipment and materials) or the money with which to buy them. The worker owns no property, and cannot survive except by working for a capitalist. Having sold his labour, the worker has no claim over the product, which belongs to his capitalist employer. The worker remains poor and dependent, while the capitalist becomes ever richer.

The relation between capital and labour is structural not personal; the worker is not oppressed by a particular capitalist but by capital, by the impersonal working of the economic system. Capital is produced by labour, but it acts as an alien force which oppresses the workers who have produced it. In the terms that Marx used in 1844, labour is 'alienated' or 'estranged'.

At this stage in the development of his ideas, Marx was strongly influenced by Ludwig Feuerbach, a materialist philosopher and critic of Hegel. In particular, Marx used the very Feuerbachian idea of a human 'essence' or 'species-being'. Human production is by nature a creative activity, and the subordination of production to the impersonal laws of capital violates the natural relation between producer and product. How far these concepts survive in Marx's mature works is controversial. The terminology of the later works is different, but the ideas of 1844 can be read into them by those who wish to do so.

In the following year, 1845, Marx and Engels worked jointly on another manuscript, also not published in their lifetime, *The German Ideology*. It represents the first definite statement of 'historical materialism' (as its authors called their theory of history), and marks the end of the first period of Marx's intellectual evolution, the period in which his ideas were changing rapidly. From 1845 on he worked to develop the basic framework set out in *The German Ideology*. It is a difficult book to read, since its positive arguments are intertwined with interminable attacks on other writers. The (later) preface to *A Contribution to the Critique of Political Economy* (discussed in appendix two below) is a better short statement of historical materialism.

In *The German Ideology*, Marx and Engels start from a simple material fact. To live, human beings must produce the means of subsistence (food, etc.), and to do so they must work together in a division of labour. (Note that no concept of an 'essence' of man is involved, beyond the material need for food.) Any stage of development of production is itself a product of history, of the achievements of past generations. The development of production necessarily involves development of forms of co-operation, of the division of labour, and hence of social organization.

Society evolves through a succession of stages, marked by different forms of property. Communal property in the ancient world was based on the exploitation of slaves, feudal landownership on the exploitation of serfs, and bourgeois (capitalist) private property on the exploitation of a proletariat of propertyless wage-workers. Each of these modes of production represents a higher stage of development of production than its predecessors, and each generates the conditions for the next. The development of capitalism creates an ever larger, increasingly impoverished, proletariat, and the proletariat will, in due course, overthrow capitalism. Communism is the inevitable end product of history.

The events of 1848 marked a watershed in Marx's life. Starting in France, popular demonstrations and uprisings spread across Europe. In the Prussian territories the popular demand was for a new constitution that would limit the arbitrary power of the autocracy, a 'revolutionary' demand at the time. A congress was set up at Frankfurt to draw up a new constitution. These events were not so much 'revolutions', in the sense of sudden and decisive changes; instead they opened a period of political turmoil in which the old regimes seemed to be tottering, and new opportunities opened up.

The *Communist Manifesto*, discussed in appendix two below, was written immediately before the outbreak of revolution, for the Communist League. In 1848, Marx was able to return to Germany, where he counselled moderation, on the grounds that Germany had first to go through an equivalent of the French revolution of 1789 before conditions could be ripe for a communist revolution. As it turned out, the radical forces in Germany became divided, the army remained loyal to the autocracy, and the Prussian government was able in the end to reassert its control. Marx went into exile again, this time in London.

2. Classical political economy

The main product of Marx's years in exile in England was *Capital*. To set *Capital* in context calls for a review of the economic theories of the time, and in particular of what Marx called 'classical political economy', the work of Adam Smith, David Ricardo and other British economists of the late eighteenth and early nineteenth centuries. Marx built on their work, and frequently refers to them.

Surplus and surplus-value

Classical political economy came into existence in opposition to the theories of the 'mercantilist' school of the seventeenth and eighteenth centuries. The mercantilists were mainly concerned with foreign trade, which Marx regarded as a secondary issue. They thought of the typical capitalist as a merchant whose profit came from buying cheap and selling dear. The first steps away from this view were taken by the French 'physiocrats' of the eighteenth century who emphasized production instead of trade, but who thought that only agriculture was truly productive. Marx studied the works of both mercantilists and physiocrats, and refer to them from time to time.

A main theme in classical political economy (and in the work of the physiocrats) was the explanation of profit and rent in terms of a *surplus* that arises from production. The basic idea can be seen most easily by imagining an economy in which only one good, say corn, is produced. Corn then serves both as a consumer good (as food) and as an input in production (as seed corn). If enough corn is produced to replace the seed and to feed the producers, any extra is a surplus, which could support a non-producing ruling class and their hangers-on (soldiers, servants, priests, etc.).

The interesting question here is: how does the surplus fall into the hands of a ruling class? The existence of a physical surplus is, of course, no answer, since a physical surplus could be enjoyed by the producers themselves. Smith, Ricardo and Marx all gave essentially the same answer to this question. In a capitalist society, the surplus is captured by property owners because they are rich enough to buy the necessary means of production (land and seed corn, in the simple example), while workers cannot afford to set up in production on their own and must accept what wages they can get. Competition for jobs between workers keeps wages at a minimum. Smith and Ricardo regarded this state of affairs as a natural eternal fact of life. Marx regarded it as a temporary stage of social development.

A further question has to be considered. In a real capitalist system many different goods are produced by specialist firms. Each firm lays out money to buy means of production and to pay wages, and it recoups its outlay by selling its product. One can talk of a physical surplus for the system as a whole, but not for each individual firm. The profit of any particular firm depends on the prices it pays and the price it gets for its product. The prices of goods may vary from week to week or day to day, so the classical economists worked with a concept of the 'normal' or 'natural' price, or '*value*' of each good. The surplus accrues to capitalists or landowners as *surplus-value*, the excess of value produced over the value absorbed by costs, including wages. A theory of surplus-value has two elements: a theory of value, and an explanation of how the surplus is extracted from workers and transferred to property owners.

Adam Smith

Adam Smith, author of *The Wealth of Nations* (1776), is generally recognized as the founder of classical political economy. He placed particular emphasis on the *division of labour* as the cause of increasing productivity and prosperity. The division of labour allows each producer to specialize and to perform particular tasks more efficiently. It is limited by the extent of the market, since small markets do not provide much scope for specialization. As wealth and population grow, and as transport methods are improved, so markets expand, allowing a more elaborate division of labour and thus greater output and wealth. Economic growth is a cumulative process, in which each step widens markets and provides a basis for further growth. Marx found the idea of a continuing process of economic development in Smith, and made it a cornerstone of his own analysis of capitalism.

The 'natural' price of any product, according to Smith, is such that it covers wage costs and rents and yields profits at the going market rate. He provided an excellent analysis of the market forces that tend to bring the price of any product into line with its 'natural' price. If the market price is high then profits will be high, producers will be attracted into that line of business, supply will be expanded and price forced down again. So far, so good, and Marx took over much of this analysis.

Smith's treatment of the determinants of wages, profits and rents is more questionable. Values, he says, are determined by adding up wages, profits and rents, but at the same time, wages, profits and rents depend on the total amount of value that has been produced and that is available to be divided between them. The argument is circular. Smith's theory of profit is very weak anyway. He says that profits are determined by 'competition', but provides no coherent analysis of how this comes about

David Ricardo

David Ricardo, a stockbroker and member of the British parliament, was the other main figure of classical political economy. His *Principles of Political Economy and Taxation* (1817) was an attempt to sort out Smith's confusions within a basically Smithian framework.

The value of a commodity, according to Ricardo, is determined by the labour required to produce it (with some exceptions, noted below). A change in wages does not change values, but it does change the fraction of the value produced that goes to wages as opposed to profits. If wages go up, profits go down, and the sum stays the same. The value of output can be measured independently of the way it is divided up.

Given this principle, difficulties still remain. The return on a given sum of money invested must be the same in different industries, since otherwise capital would flow to the more profitable investments, as Smith had explained. Where large amounts of capital are invested, relative to labour employed, a higher profit share and hence a higher price is needed to yield an acceptable return on the capital involved. Prices, therefore, cannot be proportional to labour required, after all. Ricardo puzzled over the problem, but could find no good way of solving it except to treat it as a minor modification of his labour theory of value. He ended up, then, arguing that values are mostly determined by labour except when they are not, which really amounts to abandoning labour values and collapsing back to Smith's position.

Marx criticized Ricardo for this failing, and offered his own solution, which involved treating 'values' and 'natural prices' ('prices of production', in Marx's terms) as quite different things. Values are determined by embodied labour, as a matter of definition. Wages and profits are determined by dividing up the value produced for the whole economy, and then prices of production are determined by adding up wages and profits for each good separately, following Smith. The circularity is avoided (though Marx's solution raises its own problems).

Rent remains to be explained. According to Ricardo, rent arises because different plots of land are of different fertility. The price of agricultural products must be high enough for the worst land in use to yield profit to the farmer at the going rate, since it would not be cultivated if it did not. Better land will command rent, since farmers will compete to use it, and the owner can demand rent for it. Marx took this theory over, improved it, and relegated it to the very end of *Capital*, since he regarded rent as a secondary issue.

Marx considered Smith and Ricardo to be the best representatives of political economy. After Ricardo, those economists who did not simply copy his ideas tended to emphasize 'supply and demand' as the determinants of prices. This enabled them to tell plausible stories about particular markets, but left them with no coherent analysis of wages, profits and rents for the system as a whole. Marx referred to them as 'vulgar economists' and treated them with contempt. It is, in fact, possible to give a coherent account of a whole economic system in terms of supply and demand, as was shown by Walras in the 1870s, but by that time Marx's health was failing and he seems not to have been aware of Walras's work. He would probably not have approved of it if he had known it.

Money

Completeness requires a brief discussion of monetary economics, which evolved in relative isolation from theories of value and surplus-value. Money, in Marx's time, was based on gold (at least in Britain and other major capitalist centres). Gold coins circulated and banknotes were convertible into gold. According to Marx, the value of money was directly linked to the value of gold, which depended on the labour required to produce gold (by extracting it from gold mines), just like the value of any other commodity. In this he differed from the prevailing 'quantity theory of money', which linked the value of money to the quantity in circulation. According to the quantity theory, the quantity of money determined its value. According to Marx it was the other way round; the value of money determined the amount in circulation.

Monetary debates in the mid-nineteenth century centred on the effects of the issue of banknotes. The notes concerned were not the inconvertible, government issue, paper money of today, but were promises to pay, issued by privately owned banks and redeemable in gold. The 'currency school' favoured limits on the issue of notes, since overissue might lead to price increases followed by a financial crisis. The 'banking school' saw no such danger, on the grounds that any excess issue of notes would be returned to the issuing bank to be deposited or converted into gold. On this point Marx supported the banking school; he thought that financial crises were symptoms of more fundamental problems that had nothing to do with any over-issue of notes.

3. The making of *Capital*

The development of Marx's economics

In the 1840s Marx arrived at a distinctive view of history, and of capitalism as a distinct kind of economic system with a limited life-span. At that stage, however, he took his economic theory over ready-made from others, and reinterpreted it to fit into his system. The economic sections of the *Economic and Philosophic Manuscripts* of 1844 consist mainly of quotations from Smith and others, with Marx's comments. *Wage Labour and Capital* (published 1849, based on lectures given in 1846–7) is still mainly Smithian in its over-all structure, though Marx was selective in what he took from Smith. *Wage Labour and Capital* is sometimes recommended as an easy alternative to *Capital*, but in fact presents a rather different theory. It has to be read with special caution, since Engels doctored it, after

Marx's death, to give it a superficial resemblance to Marx's mature work. *The Poverty of Philosophy* (1847) quotes extensively from Ricardo, and also from the 'Ricardian socialists', a group of radical English writers.

In the 1850s, in exile in London, Marx turned to economics again. The main evidence about the development of his ideas at this time is a manuscript written in 1857–8 which was exhumed and published in 1933 with the title *Grundrisse* (foundations). It was obviously not intended for publication, and is very difficult to read because it jumps from one subject to another with no clearly defined plan. Chaotic as it is, the *Grundrisse* contains all the main themes of *Capital*, though some are hardly developed at all, and others emerge as the manuscript proceeds. The middle and later 1850s, then, saw the development of Marx's mature economics. The interest of the *Grundrisse* to modern readers does not lie in the economics, which is much better presented in *Capital*, but in the philosophical commentary that is interwoven with it. The *Grundrisse* is much more overtly Hegelian than *Capital*, and constitutes a bridge between *Capital* and Marx's earlier philosophical works.

The next task was to find a way of presenting the new theory. Marx evidently found this very difficult. He started immediately, but *A Contribution to the Critique of Political Economy*, published in 1859, was no more than a first installment. It was a great disappointment to his friends since it dealt only with exchange and with money, and said nothing about the capital–labour relation at all. In letters to Engels, Marx sketched out a plan for the presentation of his ideas; there were to be six volumes, on capital, landed property, wage-labour, the state, international trade and the world market. The first of these became, of course, *Capital*, and grew to three volumes (plus three more volumes of *Theories of Surplus-Value*); it was never finished, and the remaining five were never even started.

'Capital'

Most of the work of writing *Capital* was done in the mid-1860s. Marx worked on drafts of all three volumes, as well as a fourth 'volume' on the history of economic ideas (large enough to fill three volumes when it was finally published under the title of *Theories of Surplus Value*). His procedure was to start with a number of very rough drafts on each topic, often copying out extracts from other writers and from factual sources, parliamentary reports and the like. In successive drafts, he would reorder the material and eliminate most of the quotations, except where they provided factual evidence or illustrated an important point. In the unfinished parts of volumes two and three, traces of these early drafts remain in the published version. In volume one, Marx made a special point of acknowledging the contributions of his predecessors by quoting the earliest statement that he could find of each important idea. (These footnote quotations can be quite puzzling to a reader unaware of their purpose).

Marx spent a long time working out the structure of *Capital*, and the result is quite unlike the *Grundrisse*. Each concept in turn is introduced, explained and defined. This arrangement, however, has its own drawbacks. As Marx wrote in the 'afterword' to the second German edition of volume one: 'Of course the method of presentation must differ in form from that of inquiry. The latter has to appropriate the material in detail . . . Only after this work is done, can the actual movement be adequately described. If this is done successfully . . . then it may appear as if we had before us a mere *a priori* construction.'

The problems Marx faced in developing and presenting his analysis of capitalism derive from the stringent requirements of his theory of history. In terms of that theory, capitalism is the latest of a succession of distinct 'modes of production'. Each mode of production is defined by a specific basic structure of the relations of production involving two classes, exploiters and exploited. All of the major features of a society are shaped (but not wholly determined) by the dominant mode of production. Each mode has its own inherent laws of motion, which serve to preserve or 'reproduce' the basic structure of the system up to a certain stage of development, but which lead eventually to its replacement by the next mode in the sequence.

To fit his analysis of capitalism into this framework, Marx had to identify the basic structure of capitalism, and derive the laws of motion of the system from it. The theory in its developed form, must move 'from the abstract to the concrete', from the abstract concept of capitalism to the actual workings of particular capitalist societies.

The 'method of inquiry' or process of research cannot, however, follow this pattern. Abstract concepts are not self-validating. They can only be tested by seeing whether they serve to describe the 'actual movement'. They do not spring fully armed from the theorist's head, but are developed by a painful process of trial and error, through the study, absorption and criticism of existing theories, and through a constant interplay between theory and evidence.

The 'method of presentation' wipes out the record of the long struggles of the 'method of inquiry'. The presentation moves from abstract to concrete, from basic concepts to elaborated theories. The concepts seem to have a life of their own, unfolding their implications step by step, and it can indeed seem 'as if we had before us a mere *a priori* construction', a product of pure abstract thought. There is a danger of falling into Hegelian idealism, of thinking that reality is *governed* by thought because it can be *reconstructed* in thought. Marx, of course, avoids this trap, and asks only that 'the actual movement be adequately *described*' (emphasis added). Modern readers of *Capital* are more likely to make the opposite mistake, and reject the theory as an arbitrary set of definitions. Patience is needed to follow Marx to the point where the theory is sufficiently developed to be applied to real world problems.

Two particular aspects of Marx's order of presentation deserve comment. Firstly, he stressed the specificity of capitalist relations of production. Capitalism (production by wage-labourers employed by capital) is a particular form of commodity production (production of goods for sale), which is itself only one form of human society. Marx distinguishes very carefully between those concepts which apply to all societies, those which apply to commodity production, and those which only apply to capitalism. He devotes the first three chapters of *Capital* to commodity production, before introducing the concept of capital for the first time. This ordering has important consequences for the way in which concepts are presented. Value, for example, is defined in the first chapter and plays a fundamental role in the analysis throughout. It cannot be related to market prices until the actual formation of prices in a capitalist system is discussed, and that is not until volume three.

Secondly, Marx's presentation is logical, not historical. The main characteristics of capitalism are determined by its structure, not its history. The origins of capitalism are not discussed until the end of volume one, while its future overthrow is only mentioned in passing. *Capital* is a study of the capitalist mode of production, not a general compendium of Marx's views.

The first volume of *Capital* was completed and published in 1867. Marx's health was poor, his time was taken up with immediate political issues, and he made almost no further progress with volumes two and three. When Marx died in 1883, Engels was left to 'make something' of a mass of almost illegible manuscripts from the 1860s. Volume two was pieced together from a number of partial drafts, and published in 1885, a commendably rapid job of editing in the circumstances. Engels, too, was ageing, and he found volume three a harder task, since it was in an even less finished state. It finally appeared in 1894, thirty years after it was written.

4. The economic background

Capital is primarily a work of theory, intended to provide the basis for an analysis of any capitalist economy at any date. Marx drew his examples, of course, from his own time, and assumptions appropriate to the time play an important role in the more theoretical sections of the work. In particular, Marx took it for granted that individual capitalist firms were relatively small, and had little or no control over the prices of their products; they had to sell at the market price or not at all. A system of very large, monopolistic producers would have to be analysed differently; Marx predicted the emergence of large enterprises, but the task of modifying the theory was left to his successors. Marx's monetary theory is also very much rooted in the nineteenth century; for him, money is based on gold.

Capital is very much easier to understand if the reader is aware of the ways in which the economy of Marx's time differed from that of today. Most of Marx's examples come from Britain; as he explained to his German readers, England was the 'classic ground' of capitalism, the first capitalist nation and at that time the most advanced and best documented. (Like many Germans, Marx habitually said 'England' when he meant Britain; many of his examples come from Scotland.)

Capitalist production is defined by the employment of wage-labour to work with materials and equipment provided by the capitalist. This form of organization was dominant in Britain in the mid-nineteenth century, but almost nowhere else. Even the northern United States was predominantly a country of small farmers. In Britain, a large part of output was produced by individual 'self-employed' workers, together with those who worked in their own homes on an 'outwork' basis, depending on a merchant to provide materials and buy the product. Industries like cotton-textiles, in which factory production using steam power predominated, were the exception rather than the rule. When Marx described 'modern industry', he was describing something quite novel.

Britain was the richest and most advanced capitalist nation, but it was still poor by modern standards. There is little point in trying to make exact comparisons with modern conditions, but there can be no dispute that hours of work were long and wages desperately low, as is shown by the evidence that Marx quotes.

Businesses were small by modern standards. Firms were usually controlled by an individual (or family, or partnership) who controlled the business directly, and personally confronted the workers on the factory floor. Each individual capitalist had little or no control over his markets, and had to sell at the going price or not at all. There was a genuine difficulty in explaining why competition did not eliminate profits altogether. Marx's theory of surplus-value is designed to answer this question. A few large scale capitalist businesses, notably railways, were organized as joint-stock companies (corporations) with transferable shares and a professional management. They showed something of what was to come, but Marx expected the downfall of capitalism to cut short this line of development.

Agriculture was still the largest industry in Britain, and Britain was almost unique in the nineteenth-century world in that agriculture was substantially organized on capitalist lines, with landowners collecting rent, agricultural wage-workers doing the work, and capitalist farmers standing between the two. According to Marx, the creation of capitalist agriculture by the expulsion of peasant farmers played a crucial role in the emergence of industrial capitalism.

The monetary system, both in Britain and in much of the rest of the world, was based on gold. Privately owned banks issued notes, which were simply promises to pay a given sum on demand. Bank of England notes still say 'I promise to pay the bearer on demand the sum of . . . ', over the signature of the chief cashier, but that is now an empty form of words; in Marx's time it was not. The Bank of England was then privately owned and stood at the centre of the monetary system, thanks to its longstanding position as the government's banker. Its notes circulated throughout the country, and were convertible into gold. Marx frequently describes sums of money in terms of the British currency of the time. The pound sterling (£) was divided into twenty shillings (s), each further divided into twelve pence (d; singular: one penny). For example, 6s 8d is one third of a pound.

Transactions between capitalist firms were largely carried out through 'bills of exchange', a system that is much less used now. When Marx talks of the 'credit system' it is this that he has in mind. When A sold goods to B, he might give credit by writing a 'bill', a demand for payment on a specified future date, which B would 'accept' by signing it. Instead of waiting for his money, A might pass the bill to someone else to whom he owed money (so that bills circulated to a degree in place of money), or he might sell the bill to a bank. By taking over the bill, the bank would be lending money until the bill was paid, and would deduct interest; this was called 'discounting' a bill. Firms often arranged for their bills to be paid by a London bank, and the bills often ended up in London banks too, so bills could often be settled by cancelling them off against each other in London with no actual money changing hands. This is why Marx often speaks of the credit system as a way of economizing on the use of money. Bills have since been almost entirely superseded by the transfer of bank deposits by cheque, a system that Marx hardly mentions. Modern economists treat bank deposits as a form of money; Marx never does.

Marx encountered developed capitalism in Britain as an adult. He grew up in Trier, which was at that time a country town almost untouched by the development of industrial capitalism. One of the first economic issues that he wrote about was the right of peasants to collect firewood in the forests; in Prussia in 1836, almost three-quarters of penal proceedings concerned trespassing, poaching and the like. For Marx, the development of capitalism from earlier forms of society was not a purely historical question. In Western Europe as a whole, capitalism was much less developed than in Britain. Factory production was less widespread, merchants played a larger role, and peasant agriculture predominated. Nevertheless it was clear to Marx, if not to many of his contemporaries, that capitalist Britain showed the way that the whole of Europe was going.

Other parts of the world were even further from the pure model of capitalism set out in *Capital*. Slavery, in the United States, and serfdom, in Russia, persisted into the 1860s when *Capital* was written. In India and China, yet another mode of production prevailed, which Marx called the 'Asiatic' mode. (Subsequent research has cast doubts on Marx's picture of Asiatic societies.) African society was virtually unknown in Europe in Marx's time. Marx's confident assertion that the whole world would first be transformed by capitalism, then by socialism, was an extraordinary leap of the imagination in the times in which he lived.

VOLUME 1

Capitalist production

PART 1

Commodities and money

The first few chapters of *Capital* are notoriously the hardest to understand. Part of the difficulty is caused by Marx's style, which is more 'Hegelian', and therefore more obscure, than in later chapters. A more substantial problem is that he tries to introduce each concept in turn, and to define it rigorously, before moving on. This is an almost impossible task (what concepts do you use to define the first concept?), and makes the early parts of *Capital* seem very abstract. In the very first chapter Marx discusses 'value in exchange' without any consideration of the actual process of exchange; in the second chapter, exchange comes first, and money only later. The concepts defined in early parts of the book cannot be fully understood until they have been put to use later on. Perhaps it is best, on a first reading, to go through the early chapters rather briskly, and to return to them later.

Chapter 1. Commodities

Section 1. The two factors of a commodity: use-value and value

A capitalist system has two defining features. Firstly, it is a *commodity producing* system, that is, a system in which goods are produced for sale. Secondly, it is *capitalist*, in that production is controlled by capitalists who employ workers. To begin with, Marx considers only the first aspect; workers and capitalists do not appear for several chapters. Money, too, is kept in the background at first, so

21

exchange is presented as if one good were directly exchanged for another.

A commodity is defined as something that is exchanged for other commodities.

All commodities are *use-values*, that is, they satisfy some want or need, directly or indirectly. The nature of the wants involved is irrelevant at this stage, and no moral judgement is implied; weapons satisfy a 'need' in a warlike society, and hence cound as use-values, and so on.

Commodities also possess *exchange-value*, the property of being exchangeable for other things.

The distinction between use-value and exchange-value is the first of a series of distinctions that Marx maintains rigorously throughout *Capital*, between those aspects of human life that are common to all societies, and those that are specific to a particular kind of society. All societies produce use-values of some kind or other, since there are human needs, for food, shelter, and so on, that must be met. The institution of exchange, however, is only found in some societies, and it is only in these societies that commodities are produced. Without exchange, there is, of course, no exchange-value. All commodities must possess use-value, because no-one would buy them if they did not, but there are many things that are use-values but are not exchanged and therefore never become commodities.

Exchange establishes a quantitative (numerical) relation between different commodities; x units of one commodity exchange for y units of another. For quantitative comparisons of this sort to be possible, Marx asserts, both commodities must 'contain' some common substance, which he calls *value* (with no qualifier attached). The common substance cannot be any physical property, such as weight, since physical properties pertain to the use-value aspect of the commodity, so the common factor can only be that both are the product of *labour*. The labour that is the substance of value, Marx calls 'abstract' labour (discussed further in the next section). His argument is not very convincing as it stands, and the 'labour theory of value' must be justified by the use that Marx makes of it in his system as a whole.[1]

Marx next discusses the magnitude of value; how much value

does a commodity contain? The value of any commodity, he says, depends on the quantity of *socially necessary labour* embodied in it, that is, the *labour-time* required to produce it 'under the normal conditions of production, and with the average degree of skill and intensity prevalent at the time' (p. 39).[2] The value of a particular item does not depend on the hours of actual work that went into that particular example, but on the hours that are 'socially necessary'; value is social, not individual. A slow worker produces less value than a faster one. 'Value' is a wholly technical term, with no ethical content. If a bomb and a painting are produced by equal amounts of (socially necessary) labour, then they have equal values; there is no assertion that they are equally desirable in any moral sense. Marx does not, incidentally, explain how the value of a commodity can be calculated if it is produced jointly with another as, for example, wool and mutton are jointly produced by rearing sheep. How much labour should be attributed to the production of the wool, and how much to the mutton?

Section 2. The two-fold character of the labour embodied in commodities

The distinction between use-value and exchange-value can now be elaborated into a distinction between two aspects of labour: *useful labour* and *abstract labour*. Useful labour is labour that produces use-values. It is an 'eternal nature-imposed necessity' (pp. 42–3) in all societies. Corresponding to the many different kinds of use-values that are produced, there are many different, specific kinds of useful labour involved in producing them. In a commodity producing society there is a complex *division of labour* between different individuals doing different kinds of work, who exchange their products. Without a division of labour there would be no commodity production or exchange, since the only point of exchange is to trade one commodity for a different one. However, useful labour could, in principle, go on without any division of labour (Robinson Crusoe with no Man Friday), and a division of labour can exist without products being exchanged on a market (in a self-sufficient commune, for example). Marx reserves the phrase *social division of labour* for the division between independent producers who sell their products to each other as opposed to that within, say, a family, or a factory, or a primitive tribe. He also points out that nature as well as labour is necessary for the production of use-values; there is no suggestion that labour is the unaided source of wealth in the sense of use-values.

In a commodity producing society, however, different kinds of useful labour have the common feature that they produce exchange-value. In so far as labour produces value, it is called *abstract labour*, the 'expenditure of human brains, nerves, and muscles . . . human labour in general' (p. 44) regardless of which use-value is produced. (A use-value of some sort must be produced, since a commodity cannot have exchange-value without use-value.)

Skilled labour is a problem. Marx argues that skilled labour counts as multiplied simple labour, so that (say) one hour of skilled work might count as two hours of simple, abstract labour. The key question is, obviously, what determines how much simple labour is equivalent to an hour of a particular sort of skilled labour. Marx claims that this equation is no problem, since it is constantly made in practice 'by a social process that goes on behind the backs of the producers' (p. 44) through the exchange of the products of skilled labour for the products of unskilled labour. (Wages, of course, have not come into the story at all yet.) The argument is circular (values are determined by labour content, while equivalent labour content is computed from observed exchange-values) and has been the subject of criticism.[3]

The value of a commodity is not fixed for all time, or inherent in the commodity itself. If the productiveness of labour increases, less labour will be (socially) necessary to produce a particular object, and its value will fall. Put another way, the value created by an hour of average labour is always the same, though the amount of use-values produced in the hour may change.

The status of the concept of value set out here is unclear. Is it something real (in some sense) that Marx claims to have discovered, or delineated more accurately than his predecessors, or is it a concept that he has invented and defined in order to analyse capitalism? The text can be read either way.

In any case, Marx does *not* assert that goods actually exchange in ratios proportional to their relative values. If, say, a bushel of wheat and a coat contain the same amount of socially necessary labour, and hence have the same value, it does not follow that they will exchange one for one in practice. In the main theoretical parts of the first two volumes, Marx explicitly *assumes* that prices are proportional to values, as a simplification, and in volume three, part two, he goes on to explain how prices are related to values. In the first two volumes there are occasional, rather informal, discussions of the deviation of market-price ratios from value ratios.

Section 3. The form of value or exchange-value

Marx next discusses the way value is expressed in the exchange-value of commodities. He starts with the simple equivalence of two commodities and works up to the expression of values in terms of money prices. A major difficulty in reading the section is to see what all the fuss is about, and why Marx spends so long on the question. It may be that he felt an obligation to spell his procedure out very thoroughly because the search for an 'invariable standard' of value was of great concern to economists of his time (or, more accurately, to those of the previous generation). The issue is largely forgotten today, and Marx's main points are really simpler than they look.

It is important to remember that any deviation of actual prices from values is ignored here. Marx is concerned with the *qualitative* problem of what exchange-values are and the units in which they are to be measured, and not with the *quantitative* issue of exactly how much of one good is traded for another.

Marx first takes an equation between the values of two commodities (20 yards of linen equals one coat), and distinguishes the *relative form of value* (the equation measures the value of linen relative to something else) from the *equivalent form of value* (the coat serves here as a unit of measurement of values). They can be interchanged (one coat equals 20 yards of linen). Labour, the substance of value, does not appear on either side, because an exchange is always an exchange *of one commodity for another*, so the value of a commodity can only be observed in terms of its relation to the value of another commodity. A particular commodity has a use-value in its own right, but it only has exchange-value in relation to other commodities. The value of linen in terms of coats may change because the value of linen has changed, or because the value of coats has changed, or both.

Towards the end of the discussion of the 'elementary or accidental form of value', Marx comments that 'the elementary value-form is also the primitive form under which a product of labour appears historically as a commodity . . . ' (p. 61). Marx's presentation is arranged in an order dictated by the logic of the theory, but in some (only some) cases he hints that the historical development followed the same order.[4] The idea here is that exchange first emerged as the isolated and occasional barter of particular products.

In a developed commodity producing system, anything is exchangeable for anything else. Marx proceeds via the 'expanded relative form of value', to the 'general form of value', in which the value of all commodities except one is expressed in terms of the remaining commodity, the 'universal equivalent'. In practice, some particular commodity is socially identified as the universal equivalent, and serves as *money*. Marx assumes that money will be a commodity in its own right, with its own value as a product of labour. In Marx's time gold served as monetary standard, and he regards paper money unbacked by gold as a deviation from the norm. Money is not usually backed by gold (or anything else) today.

Section 4. The fetishism of commodities

Marx next turns to a quite different question. He intends not only to explain how the capitalist system works, but also to explain both why it needs explaining, why it is not immediately obvious how the system works, and how people come to form the (inadequate) understanding of the system that they do have. The basic point is that a commodity producing system is obscure, because (economic) relations between people are carried out by the buying and selling of things. Each individual is concerned only with the things that are bought and sold. The transposition of *social* properties onto *material things* is what Marx calls *fetishism* (referring to religious cults that attribute supernatural powers to some material object, a fetish). Marx returns to this theme throughout *Capital*, but with tantalizing brevity.

Commodity production presupposes a social division of labour in which each individual depends on many others. Once it is well established, the value of different commodities appears to be an inherent property of the commodities themselves, and the social basis of value is obscured. Money appears to be the 'natural' incarnation of value. (Marx's rather tedious construction of money as a particular form of the value relation, presented in the preceding section, is designed to dispel this illusion.)

Marx does not altogether deny the validity of the impressions formed in everyday life. 'The relations connecting the labour of one individual with that of the rest appear, not as direct social relations between individuals at work, but as *what they really are*, material relations between persons and social relations between things' (p. 73). 'The categories of bourgeois economy . . . are forms of thought expressing *with social validity* the conditions and relations of a definite, historically determined mode of production' (p. 76) (emphasis added in both quotations). It is not that people are blind or stupid, but that they see the world from a certain angle, in terms of their direct experience, and as a result their understanding of the world is limited and inadequate.

Other modes of production are easier to understand, partly because they are inherently less confusing, partly because we see them from the outside. In the feudal societies of the middle ages, for example, the labour performed by a serf on the lord's estate was perfectly visible, and no-one could be in any doubt as to what was going on. Comparisons between different societies designed to show that capitalism is not natural or eternal but is instead a specific, historically limited form of organization are another recurrent theme in *Capital*.

Looking back over the main themes of this first chapter, Marx's aims can already be seen in outline. Firstly, he will show how the economic system works in terms of the actual material process of producing use-values. Secondly, he will show how the production of use-values is controlled by the process of producing exchange-values (or, in a fully capitalist society, surplus-value or profit) and he will explain exchange-value and surplus-value as the result of a particular, historically specific form of social organization. Thirdly, he will explain how the economy appears to the individuals actually involved. Fourthly (this has hardly surfaced so far) he will trace the historical origins of capitalism and its subsequent development, and he will project that development forward to predict the overthrow of capitalism and its replacement by socialism.

Chapter 2. Exchange

The exchange of commodities is a transaction between the owners of commodities. In the first chapter, Marx treated commodities as being exchangeable, in the abstract, without any discussion of the actual process of exchange. He now repairs the omission.

The owner of commodities parts with things he does not want to consume, that are not use-values for him, in exchange for commodities that meet his needs.

Exchange can only take place if each party recognises the other as the owner of the commodities to be traded. Private, individual ownership is a prerequisite or, better, a concomitant of exchange (the two grew up together). In simple societies with common ownership of products, exchange takes place between separate communities. Later it penetrates inside the community, common ownership breaks down, and exchange between individuals in the same community emerges. To begin with, there are isolated exchanges motivated by particular, transient surpluses and shortages, not regulated by the law of value. Value becomes the regulating principle as commodity production becomes the dominant form of organization. As commodity ownership and exchange become universal and regular, it becomes a practical necessity that values be measured in some socially accepted universal equivalent. Money therefore emerges. It is futile to blame social problems on money or to propose to eliminate money without eliminating commodity exchange (as some 'socialist' reformers of Marx's time did). Money is a necessary concomitant of exchange, and the one cannot be abolished without the other.

Precious metals are particularly suited to the role of money commodity, because they are uniform and divisible. Marx again stresses that gold is a commodity like others; it does not have value because it is used as money, but because labour is required to produce it.

Chapter 3. Money, or the circulation of commodities

Section 1. The measure of value

When money is used as a *measure of value*, no actual gold need be present (just as, for example, we can say that an object is a foot long without having a foot ruler to hand). Nevertheless, the value of a commodity is expressed in terms of a physical quantity of gold. For example, a ton of iron may have the same value as (contain as much labour as) two ounces of gold. For this equation to be possible, gold must itself have value.

In practice, prices or values are not quoted in ounces of gold, but in conventional units such as pounds sterling, dollars, francs, and so on. In a gold based system the *standard of price* (say, the pound sterling) is a name given to a particular physical quantity of gold, and can be arbitrarily established by law. In the British money of Marx's time, an ounce of gold was equal to £3 17s 10½d, so that if a ton of iron had the same value as two ounces of gold, its value could be quoted as £7 15s 9d (= 2 × £3 17s 10½d). Changes in the value of gold do not alter the standard of price, but they do alter the value that it represents. The legal definition of a standard of price, on the other hand, does not alter the actual value of anything; it merely defines the name of the unit of measurement.

Money prices may rise or fall either because the value of the commodities concerned has changed, or because of a change in the value of gold. The price of a commodity may also deviate from the gold equivalent of its value. A commodity producing system is not controlled by any central authority, and the market mechanism necessarily involves price fluctuations. Overproduction corrects itself by bringing down prices, and so on. The point is clearer in some of Marx's early writings, in which he criticizes the idea that prices should be somehow fixed to make them correspond to values. The laws of a market system 'impose themselves only as the mean of apparently lawless irregularities that compensate one another' (p. 102).

A note on terminology here may avoid confusion later. One should not, strictly, say that a commodity has a value of £x, but that its value is equal to that contained in the amount of gold represented by £x. The substance of value is labour, not gold. Marx is some-times, but not always, careful to spell this out. A statement that prices are (or are not) equal to values, or proportional to values, should be read as saying that equal money prices correspond (or do not correspond) to equal values. As Marx has shown in chapter one, what matters is how much of one commodity exchanges for another.

Section 2. The medium of circulation

When the owner of commodities sells them and buys something else, he first gets money, then spends it; money serves as *medium of circulation*. Marx expresses this in a formula: $C - M - C$. The for-mula represents successive transformations of the value possessed by the individual, starting with commodities (C), which are exchanged for money (M), which is then in turn exchanged for a dif-ferent set of commodities (the second C). The price which a seller can get for his product is determined by competition in the market, by a social process independent of the will of any particular indi-vidual. If a commodity owner is to sell his product at all, he must find a buyer who has money to buy with. This buyer, in turn, got his money by selling his product to someone else, and so on. Each simple exchange is linked to all the others, making up the *circulation of commodities*.

After describing the circulation of commodities, Marx takes on, and rejects, Say's Law (as it has come to be called), the 'childish . . . dogma, that because every sale is a purchase, and every pur-chase a sale, therefore the circulation of commodities necessarily implies an equilibrium of sales and purchases' (p. 113). If this were true, it would mean that a general overproduction of goods (relative to demand) would be impossible, and there could be no 'crises' of the sort Marx will discuss later.

Say's Law was generally accepted by non-Marxist economists until the writings of Keynes in the 1930s, though not in quite the crude form that Marx attacks. It could not, after all, be denied that crises occurred, but they were commonly thought of as the result of some sort of interference with the smooth working of a market system, such as monetary mismanagement or mistaken regulation of wages and prices.

Marx does not, of course, deny that every actual sale is also a purchase by someone else. He simply points out that it does not follow that a would-be seller will always find a buyer. If those who have money refuse (for whatever reason) to spend it, then others will find that they cannot sell, and they in turn will not have the money to buy. The logical possibility of a general inability of producers to sell, a crisis, is thus established. As Marx emphasizes, there is a long way to go in order to establish the circumstances in which such a crisis will actually happen.

Commodities are produced and consumed outside the circulation process, which serves as a sort of conveyor belt transferring goods from producer to consumer. Meanwhile, money (the conveyor belt) circulates from hand to hand, always remaining in the process of circulation. The amount of money needed to carry out the circulation of commodities depends on the volume of exchanges (twice as much business requires twice as much money), and on the money price of commodities (if prices are doubled, twice as much money will pass from hand to hand). Later, Marx introduces the velocity of circulation, the rate at which money circulates, as an additional determinant of the required volume of circulating money. If money circulates twice as fast, then only half as much is needed to carry out a given volume of exchanges.

Suppose that the value of gold falls, because it can now be produced more cheaply. More gold will now be required to represent the same value (prices in gold will be higher), so more money will be needed in circulation. How does this come about? Initially, gold production is cheaper, but money prices remain as before. Gold production is more profitable, and more gold is produced and exchanged for other commodities. This extra demand pushes up prices, and the effects spread through the system, with higher prices and a greater volume of circulating money, until a new equilibrium is reached. The value of gold and the volume of exchanges together determine the amount of (gold) money in circulation. Marx here is attacking the 'quantity theory of money' (widely accepted then as now), in which the quantity of money in circulation determines its value. Causality, he says, runs the other way round. His argument, of course, applies only to commodity (gold) money, and not to the inconvertible paper currencies normal today.

Coins were originally simply standardized pieces of precious metal, but it is possible to replace them by token coins or by paper notes. Given government backing, notes and token coins can circulate and replace the amount of gold that would have been required in circulation. If, however, an excessive quantity of paper money is issued, its value in exchange will decline proportionately. The quantity theory, it seems, applies after all, but only to paper money, not gold.

Section 3. Money

Money can be hoarded (accumulated as a static stock of gold) without necessarily disrupting circulation, since gold is constantly being produced and can be acquired by the hoarder in exchange for other commodities. Hoards of money perform a function, since money can be released from hoards, or absorbed into them, as the needs of circulation fluctuate.

Goods can be sold on credit. In this case, payment is delayed and money is not used to buy commodities but to settle debts. Money is also used for transactions that do not involve the sale of commodities: for paying taxes, rents, and so on. When money is used to settle debts it serves as *means of payment*. It serves as *means of purchase* when commodities are bought for cash. In a system which uses credit extensively, mutual debts can be cancelled against each other, economizing on the need for cash. The transfer of bank balances by cheque is not considered; it was less important when Marx wrote than it is now.

In a monetary crisis (a stage in a more general crisis, which is not discussed fully here), cash suddenly comes into demand as lenders become unwilling to extend credit.

Inside a single country, gold money may be replaced by tokens (coins, notes) authorized by the government, but balances in international transactions must be settled in bullion, and national banks hold reserves for this purpose. Again, things have changed; various national currencies, notably US dollars, are now used instead of gold. As has already been noted, monetary practices have changed a lot since Marx's time, and the theory needs to be modified before it can be applied in modern circumstances.

PART 2

The transformation of money into capital

The three chapters that make up part two hang together as a single unit. Although they are short, they are the heart of Marx's analysis of capitalism.

Chapter 4. The general formula for capital

Marx now starts to discuss *capital*, without at first defining it. A preliminary definition emerges by the end of the chapter, though it has been said that Marx's definition of capital consists of the whole of the three volumes of *Capital*. Capital emerged first, we are told, 'from the creation in the 16th century of a world-embracing commerce and a world-embracing market', and appears first in the form of money, 'as the capital of the merchant and of the usurer' (p. 146).

The 'formula' for capital, or for the *circuit of capital*, is $M - C - M$. The capitalist starts with a sum of money (M), buys commodities (C) and sells them, to end up with money again (the second M). Marx calls the first stage ($M - C$) an *advance* of capital, and the second stage ($C - M$), the *realization* of capital.

The whole business would be pointless if the capitalist only got back the same amount of money as he started with, so Marx rewrites the formula as $M - C - M'$, where M' represents a larger sum of money than M. The additional money that the capitalist ends up with, M' minus M, Marx calls *surplus-value*. The circuit of capital is a process or activity that generates surplus-value. Marx justifies his formula by saying (at the end of the chapter) that it is 'the description of Capital from the mouths of its first interpreters, the Mercantilists' (p. 155).

The circuit of capital, $M - C - M'$, differs from that of the simple circulation of commodities, $C - M - C$, in that simple commodity circulation is aimed at the satisfaction of particular wants by the purchase of specific commodities, so it is limited by the extent of those wants. The circuit of capital, by contrast, is aimed at the quantitative expansion of money-value, a process that has no inherent limits. The capitalist aims at 'the restless, never-ending process of profit making alone' (p. 152).

'Value therefore now becomes value in process, money in process, and, as such, capital' (p. 154). Capital is value, but it is defined not by the particular stuff it is embodied in (money, commodities), but by the fact that it is involved in a particular process, the process of producing surplus-value. Marx's definition of capital is quite different from that of non-Marxist economists, who define capital as a particular set of commodities, the 'produced means of production', such as buildings, machines, and so on. Accountants and businessmen use the term in a sense closer to that of Marx. When Marx talks of a certain amount of capital (say, 'a capital of £1 million'), he is referring to a sum of value that is constantly being transformed from money to commodities and back again. He often talks of *a* capital, in the singular, to mean the capital of a particular enterprise or individual capitalist. Capitalists, incidentally, are never very fully discussed; they are simply the owners of capital.

Chapter 5. Contradictions in the general formula for capital

In defining capital by the formula $M - C - M'$, the production of surplus-value, Marx has not yet explained anything. He has merely posed a problem; where does the surplus-value come from? In chapter five he deliberately sets up a puzzle, by apparently showing that surplus-value cannot exist, and in chapter six he will resolve the difficulty.

Recall Marx's rigorous distinction between use-value and exchange-value. When commodities are exchanged, both parties gain in terms of use-value; each parts with something he does not want, and gets in exchange something that he does want. This gain, however, has nothing to do with exchange-value, and the capitalist who starts and finishes with money is interested only in exchange-value.

If equivalents are exchanged, value for value, the process $M - C - M'$ becomes $M - C - M$; there is no surplus-value to be gained by exchanging £100 for commodities, and then selling them for £100 again. If all goods are priced above (below) their values, the capitalist's gain (loss) as a seller is exactly offset by his loss (gain) as a buyer. Marx lays down as a rule for himself that 'the conversion of money into capital has to be explained on the basis of . . . the exchange of equivalents' (p. 166). He seems to have painted himself into a corner, but wait . . .

Chapter 6. The buying and selling of labour-power

No surplus-value can be created either by purchase, $M - C$, or by sale, $C - M$. The only answer to Marx's puzzle is that the capitalist must buy some commodity that can create extra value, whose 'use-value possesses the peculiar property of being a source of value . . . ' (p. 167).

Such a commodity exists; it is *labour-power*, the capacity to labour, which creates value because labour is the source of value. Marx makes another crucial distinction here, between *labour*, which is an activity not a thing, and cannot be sold, and *labour-power*, which is what a worker sells when he agrees to work for a capitalist in return for a wage. The wage is the price of labour-power.

For labour-power to be for sale, there must exist *a class of free labourers*, a *proletariat* who are, Marx says, free in a 'double sense'. They are free to sell their labour-power; they are not slaves or serfs. They are also 'free' of any ownership of commodities, so that they have nothing else to sell but their labour-power. (This particular play on words comes over rather badly in English.) Proletarians cannot produce for themselves because they do not own the necessary *means of production* (materials, implements, and so on) or, which comes to the same thing, they do not have the money they would need to buy means of production and to support themselves until the returns come in.

The existence of a class of free labourers is a result of historical development, as are all the other prerequisites for the emergence of capital. After stressing this point, Marx leaves it aside; the historical emergence of capitalism and, in particular, of a proletariat, will be dealt with at length in part eight.

The *value of labour-power*, like that of any other commodity, is determined by the labour necessary for its production. In the case of labour-power, this is the labour embodied in (i.e. the value of) the commodities required for the worker's subsistence, including a 'historical and moral element' the size of which is 'in a given country, at a given period . . . practically known' (p. 171). Marx's introduction of this historical and moral element is open to criticism as question begging; it comes close to saying that the value of labour-power is whatever it happens to be. It may be above physiological subsistence, since any discrepancy can be described as due to the 'historical and moral element'.

The value of labour-power must also, Marx continues, contain an element to cover the cost of the reproduction of labour-power, that is, the raising of children to replace the labourer in due course, and, in the case of skilled labour, an element to cover the cost of training and education.

The value of labour-power should be thought of as the value of the capacity to work during a definite period. Marx usually measures labour-power in days, so he considers the value of the commodities needed to keep the worker and his family for a day. If half a day's labour embodied in commodities can serve to 'produce' a day's labour-power, so that, say, commodities embodying six hours labour suffice to fuel a worker to perform twelve hours work, a potential source of surplus-value comes into sight.

In conformity with the rule he set himself in the previous chapter, Marx generally assumes that labour-power is exchanged at its value, though the price of labour-power, like the price of anything else, may deviate from its value. The determinants of the actual market price of labour-power will emerge later; the existence of a 'reserve army' of unemployed labourers will play a crucial role in explaining why wages do not rise far above the value of labour-power.

Once the capitalist has bought labour-power (he is assumed to pay at once, though in practice wages are usually paid a week or so in arrears) he has to extract its use-value, the actual work, from the capacity to work that he has purchased. Marx ends the chapter by making an often quoted distinction between the *sphere of circulation* (or exchange) and the *sphere of production*. In circulation, the owners of commodities confront each other, in principle at least, as equals. Once the worker has sold his labour-power, he must enter the sphere of production (to which Marx now turns) and submit to the authority of the capitalist, who is entitled to control the use of the labour-power he has paid for.

PART 3

The production of absolute surplus value

In part one Marx set up a system of concepts to analyse commodity production and exchange. In part two he argued that surplus-value cannot originate in exchange, but must come about through the purchase of labour-power, and its employment in production. His next step is to analyse the capitalist production of commodities and of surplus-value. He takes a single production process operated by a single capitalist as representative of capital as a whole, and he assumes that goods exchange at their values. The title of part three, 'absolute' surplus-value, will not be explained until chapter twelve, where it is contrasted with 'relative' surplus-value.

Chapter 7. The labour-process and the process of producing surplus-value

Capitalist production can be seen in two ways: in terms of the production of use-values or in terms of the production of exchange-value and surplus-value. The two halves of chapter seven deal with them in turn.

Section 1. The labour-process or the production of use-values

Marx first discusses the *labour-process*, the activity of production, in general terms as a process of producing use-values. All societies must produce use-values (of one sort or another). Labour 'is the everlasting nature-imposed condition of human existence' (p. 184).

Human labour is purposive; a plan is first conceived in the mind, and then carried out. It differs in this, Marx says, from the activities of non-human animals such as bees or spiders (though how Marx knows about the mental processes of bees is not clear). In any case, the point here is that in a capitalist system the purpose is provided (or imposed) by the capitalist as owner of the worker's labour-power. In his early writings, Marx argued that purposive production is part of 'human nature', and that workers suffer 'alienation' in a capitalist system because their productive activity is imposed on them rather than being an expression of their own will. (See the discussion in the Introduction, above, pp. 4–5). In *Capital*, Marx avoids discussing human nature, and there have been debates over how far his approach changed between the early works and the writing of *Capital*. The emphasis on the coercive character of work in a capitalist system, and the loss of freedom that it entails, certainly persists as a *leitmotiv* throughout *Capital*.

Man operates in and on 'Nature', the natural environment, which is the ultimate source of the *subjects of labour*, the things worked on (called raw materials if they are the product of a previous labour-process). *Instruments of labour*, tools, are themselves the products of labour. Man is a tool-using animal, and different economic epochs can be distinguished archaeologically by the different kinds of tools used. Instruments and subjects of labour make up the *means of production*, and are used up in the process of *productive consumption* (as opposed to *individual consumption*, in which products such as food, clothes, and so on, are used to satisfy human needs directly).

The labour-process, as noted, is common to all forms of society. In capitalist production, labour-power and means of production are bought and set to work by the capitalist. The production process is therefore under his control, and the resulting product is his property.

Section 2. The production of surplus value

A capitalist produces use-values only because they are the necessary vehicle for the production of surplus-value. A simple numerical example (of cotton spinning) illustrates the general principles.

The value of the yarn produced is the sum of the values of the (socially necessary) means of production used up, plus the (socially necessary) labour performed in cotton spinning itself. Suppose that the value of a day's labour-power corresponds to six hours of labour (i.e. the commodities consumed by the worker and his family embody six hours of labour), and the worker is paid the equivalent in money. If he worked for six hours, the new value created (in addition to the cost of the means of production used up) would be just equal to the wage, leaving the capitalist no profit. But the labourer will be required to work for longer than this, say for twelve hours, and the extra six hours of labour will create surplus-value for the capitalist. This is the central point of Marx's theory of surplus-value. (The capitalist must, of course, ensure that only socially necessary labour is performed and that there is no slacking or waste, since wasted labour would produce no value.)

Chapter 8. Constant capital and variable capital

To produce surplus-value, the capitalist spends his money on two particular kinds of commodities; part of his capital is advanced to buy means of production, part to buy labour-power. Marx now discusses the role these two parts of capital play in the production of value and surplus-value.

The value of the means of production used up is transferred to the product (waste apart), because the labour needed to produce means of production is part of the total labour required to produce the final product. The part of capital that buys means of production, then, creates no new value or surplus-value; it is merely preserved in the value of the product and returns to the capitalist when the product is sold. Marx calls it *constant capital* because it remains constant (in value) during the process of production. The actual amount of constant capital need not, of course, stay the same from year to year, since the scale of production may alter, and so may the value of the particular items of means of production involved (as a result of technical change in the production of the means of production). Constant capital is 'constant' only in the sense that it produces no surplus-value in itself, although it is a necessary condition for the production of surplus-value. Pieces of equipment that last for a period of time are assumed to transfer their value to the product steadily during their lifetime.

Labour-power, on the other hand, is expended as actual living labour, which creates new value and surplus-value. The part of capital that is advanced to buy labour-power expands in value during the process of production, so Marx calls it *variable capital*. 'Variable' here has, of course, nothing to do with any changes from one cycle of production to the next; at this stage Marx is concerned only with what is happening to the value of the advanced capital during a single process of production

Chapter 9. The rate of surplus-value

Section 1. The degree of exploitation of labour-power

Let C stand for the capital advanced by the capitalist. It can be divided, as we have seen, into two parts; the part advanced to buy means of production is constant capital, denoted c, and the part spent on labour-power is variable capital, v. These are numerical quantities of value, represented by the equivalent sums in money, so C might, for example, be £100, with $c = $ £50 and $v = $ £50. Marx decides only to count the value of the means of production actually used up during a single period in measuring C and c. In effect, he treats production as if all means of production were used up in a single, clearly defined cycle of production. In practice this is not so, but complications arising from the different lifetimes of different pieces of equipment do not affect any important principles and can be dealt with later, when necessary.

The value of the product is $C' = c + v + s$, where s is the surplus-value produced. The new value created by labour is $v + s$, and the value of the means of production used up, c, has been transferred to the product. The capital advanced to buy labour-power, v, has expanded to $v + s$. Marx defines the *rate of surplus-value*, or *rate of exploitation*, as s/v. (The ratio of s to total capital advanced, s/C, the rate of profit, will be considered in volume three.) The symbols c, v and s, together with the ratio s/v, constitute an accounting framework which Marx will use extensively, so he runs over some numerical examples to familiarize the reader with them.

Switching attention to the working time of a representative worker, Marx divides the working day into two parts, corresponding to v and to s. The labour time in which the labourer produces a new value equal to that which he receives as the value of his labour-power, Marx calls *necessary labour*, and the remainder of the day, in which surplus-value is produced, he calls *surplus-labour*. Clearly the ratio of surplus-labour to necessary labour is equal to s/v, the rate of surplus-value

Section 2. Representation of the components of value

The total value of the product is $c + v + s$. As a matter of convenience, to provide a mental picture of what is going on, the product can be thought of as being divided into three separate parts, three heaps, corresponding in value to c, v and s, respectively.

Section 3. Senior's 'last hour'

Now, a minor diversion. Nassau Senior (a prominent English economist whose surname was Senior; it is tempting, but false, to think of him as the father of Nassau, jnr) had opposed any reduction of the working-day on the grounds that all of profit was produced in the last hour of the day. Marx gleefully demolishes him. As he has shown, a sufficient reduction of the working-day would indeed eliminate profit, but surplus-labour amounts to much more than an hour per day. Senior had overlooked the reduction in constant capital when hours, and hence output, are reduced.

Section 4. Surplus-produce

Reverting to the division of the product into parts representing c, v

and *s*, introduced in section two, Marx gives the name *surplus-produce* to the part that represents *surplus-value*.

Chapter 10. The working-day

So far, all of the elements of Marx's theory of surplus-value have been developed rigorously in terms of his theory of value, with one exception, the length of the working-day. It is precisely Marx's point that the theory of value by itself does not determine the surplus-labour extracted from the worker.

What, then, does determine the length of the working-day? It is determined by the relative strength of the two contending classes: capitalists and workers. The chapter on the working-day presents a historical account of how the fortunes of class struggle have swung first one way and then the other. A much larger and more dramatic canvas emerges than might have been expected after the rather abstract analysis of the preceding chapters. At the same time, the concepts involved here have not been given the same rigorous theoretical foundations as the strictly economic concepts used so far. The argument is much looser.

Section 1. The limits of the working-day

There are both physiological and social limits to the working-day (no-one can work twenty-four hours a day, seven days a week), but these limits are very elastic. The capitalist aims to maximize the length of the working-day and, with it, his surplus-value, while workers seek to limit it. The capitalist 'is only capital personified' and 'capital has one single life impulse . . . to absorb the greatest possible amount of surplus-labour' (p. 233). This assertion is characteristic of many that Marx makes. There is a division among Marxists between those who regard it as self-evident that capital, in the abstract, can be described in such anthropomorphic terms, and those who regard such statements as metaphors describing the consequences of a process of competition between capitalists in which each must extract the maximum surplus-value in order to survive in competition with others.

'There is here, therefore, an antinomy,' Marx continues, 'right against right . . . Between equal rights, force decides. Hence it is that in the history of capitalist production, the determination of what is a working-day, presents itself as the result of a struggle . . . between . . . the class of capitalists, and . . . the working class' (p. 235). The theme of 'right against right' is found in many of Marx's works. It is not that individual capitalists are evil people (though some particular capitalists may be), nor is it that they are doing wrong in their own terms. Workers and capitalists represent two different and incompatible interests and two codes of values. Moralizing is pointless.

Section 2. The greed for surplus-labour

Other class societies (slave systems, feudal systems), like capitalism, extract surplus-labour, but in different ways.

Section 3. Branches of English industry without legal limits to exploitation

Next, Marx gives examples of the kind of gross overwork that goes on where there are no effective limits to the working-day.

Section 4. Day and night work

In section four the examples are multiplied still further. Almost for the first time in *Capital* these discussions of the working-day reveal Marx's moral condemnation of the system he lived in, though he largely comments by implication and lets the fact speak for him.

Section 5. Compulsory laws for the extension of the working-day

From the beginnings of capitalism to the nineteenth century, the capitalist class enlisted the power of the state to enforce a lengthening of the working-day. The state, at this stage in the argument, seems rather like a *deus-ex-machina* brought in to tip the balance in the struggle of classes. Marx never fully developed his theory of the state, and in *Capital* the state only makes very sporadic appearances. Marx's whole discussion of the history of struggle over the working-day will make much more sense if it is read in conjunction with the discussion of 'primitive accumulation' in part eight.

Section 6. Compulsory limitation by law of the working-time

By the early nineteenth century, the working-day had been extended almost to the limits of what is physiologically possible, and the tide began to turn in favour of reductions in hours of work. Marx describes these struggles, and the (limited) successes they achieved in the Factory Acts in England. Through the act of 1850, 'the principle had triumphed with its victory in those great branches of industry which form the most characteristic creation of the modern mode of production. Their wonderful development from 1853 to 1860, hand-in-hand with the physical and moral regeneration of the factory workers, struck the most purblind' (p. 295). In this quotation, Marx is almost arguing against his own framework, by arguing that capitalists lost little if anything from the reduction of hours, because the quality and intensity of work improved so much.

Section 7. Reaction in other countries

The extension of the working-day, and the reaction against it, were centred in those industries that first adopted modern, mechanized methods of production. As the first modern capitalist nation, England was the first centre of that struggle, which spread throughout the world along with the spread of modern industry. Marx comments, in passing, on slavery in the USA (which had not long been abolished when he wrote): 'Labour cannot emancipate itself in the white skin where in the black it is branded' (p. 301).

Chapter 11. Rate and mass of surplus-value

Marx completes the part of *Capital* dealing with absolute surplus-value by tidying up a few loose ends. The rate of surplus-value, s/v, depends on the value of labour-power and the length of the working-day. The total, or mass, of surplus-value gained by a capitalist (or any aggregate of capitalists) is equal to s/v multiplied by v, the total variable capital, and the latter is equal to the value of an individual labour-power multiplied by the number of labourers employed. (Note that Marx uses two expressions, s/v and a'/a, for the same thing.) As long as the value of labour-power is fixed, there are limits to any increase in s/v, because the working-day cannot be expanded indefinitely.

Surplus-value is proportional to variable capital and not to total capital advanced. This proposition seems to contradict all experience, which suggests that equal capitals should yield equal profits regardless of the proportion of variable capital involved. The apparent puzzle will be resolved in volume three.

A certain minimum sum of money is needed to become a capitalist, and this minimum rises as capitalist production advances. It becomes increasingly difficult to become a capitalist.

Marx also notes that: 'At first, capital subordinates labour on the basis of the technical conditions in which it historically finds it. It does not, therefore, change immediately the mode of production' (p. 310). The technical transformations that follow this early stage of capitalism are the subject of the next part of *Capital*. The phrase 'mode of production' is clearly being used in this context to refer to the technology and organization of production in a rather general way, and Marx uses it in this sense in many places in *Capital*. In other contexts it is an important technical term with a specific meaning (as in 'capitalist mode of production'), referring to the major stages of development of the social relations of production. Modern Marxists always use the phrase in the latter sense.

PART 4

Production of relative surplus-value

So far, Marx has concentrated on the question: where does surplus-value come from? The context for this question is a generalized capitalist system, capitalism in the abstract. He now turns to *relative surplus-value*, which is the result of *changes* in the productivity of labour, and this provides the context for an examination of the historical development of capitalist production, starting from the simple technology inherited from earlier forms of society, and ending with the 'modern industry' of Marx's own time.

Chapter 12. The concept of relative surplus-value

Marx has already explained how the working-day can be thought of as divided into two parts. Necessary labour-time is that part of the day in which the worker recoups for the capitalist the value which the capitalist has paid in wages. The rest of the working-day is surplus-labour, in which the worker creates surplus-value. The rate of surplus-value can be increased by lengthening the working-day, so that more surplus-labour is extracted on top of a given amount of necessary labour.

Surplus-value can equally be increased, within the limits of a given working-day, if necessary labour-time can be reduced, that is, if the value of labour-power falls.

The value of labour-power, in turn, is the value of the commodities required to reproduce labour-power. It will fall if the productivity of labour rises in the production of these goods, so that their value falls. What is required is that 'the labour-process in the form in which it has historically been handed down' should be transformed. 'The technical and social conditions of the process, and consequently the very mode of production must be revolutionised' (p. 315). Here, as in the previous chapter, Marx is using the phrase 'mode of production' in a general sense, to refer to all aspects of the process of production.

Surplus-value that derives from a reduction in necessary labour-time is called *relative surplus-value*, distinguished from *absolute surplus-value*, which results from a lengthening of the working-day. It is not possible, of course, to identify one part of surplus-value as 'absolute' and another part as 'relative' without some starting point; these terms apply to *changes* in the rate of surplus-value from some initial position. Marx makes this point later on, in chapter sixteen.

If a capitalist forces his workers to work longer hours, he benefits directly from the resulting (absolute) surplus-value. By contrast, the effect on surplus-value of productivity increases (relative surplus-value) is more indirect. A reduction in the value of labour-power benefits all capitalists, and no individual capitalist introduces new techniques with the conscious intention of reducing the value of labour-power.

In a significant pronouncement on his intellectual strategy, Marx distinguishes between 'the laws, immanent in capitalist production' and the way they 'manifest themselves in the movements of individual masses of capital, where they assert themselves as coercive laws of competition, and are brought home to the mind . . . of the individual capitalist' (p. 316). According to Marx, the system must be analysed first, and the individual capitalist later. Although this principle is stated in the discussion of relative surplus-value, Marx intends it to be applied more widely. He is not saying that capitalism can exist without capitalists, of course; it is a matter of the order of development of the theory. It remains, perhaps, difficult to see how Marx can explain the 'laws' of capitalist production without reference to individual capitalists, and he goes on here to relax his rule and discuss the incentives that guide the actions of particular capitalists.

The value of an article depends on the labour *socially necessary* to produce it. If an individual capitalist can find a way of raising productivity above the general level, he can reap more surplus-value, since the general level of productivity still determines the value of the product. This is a strong incentive to increase productivity. Other capitalists will then be forced to copy the new methods, for fear of being undersold, and the value of the product will fall as the general level of productivity is raised. The special gain to the innovator is only temporary.

If the product concerned is part of the means of subsistence (part of the socially necessary consumption of workers), or if it is a means of production used to produce means of subsistence, the value of labour-power will fall for the whole system, and the general rate of surplus-value will be increased. Workers need not be paid so much (in value terms) to allow them to consume the same use-values.

The analysis may seem counter-intuitive (if workers are more productive, surely they produce more value?). The point hinges on Marx's strict distinction between value and use-value. A general increase in productivity means that more use-values are produced per hour but, by definition, an hour of (socially necessary) labour always produces the same value.

Chapter 13. Co-operation

Marx now discusses, in three successive chapters, three different ways in which a capitalist labour-process can be organized. These forms (*simple co-operation*, *manufacture*, and *modern industry*) form a broad historical sequence, though, as Marx notes at the end of chapter thirteen, the earlier forms continue both within and alongside more developed forms.

By *simple co-operation* Marx means the bringing together of numbers of workers who perform basically similar tasks. A number of advantages flow from a simple increase in the scale of operations. Differences between individual workers average out, and results become more predictable. There are economies in the use of buildings and other means of production, if these are shared. Workers can co-operate on tasks that would be beyond the power of any single individual.

Large scale capitalist operations are only possible if a single capitalist employs numbers of workers, so the scale of co-operation is limited by the size of the capital owned by a single capitalist. Since it is the capitalist who brings workers together, the productive powers created by co-operation appear to be the creation of capital. This is an illusion, a form of fetishism. The power of co-operation shows up equally in ancient pyramids and the like, which have nothing to do with capitalism.

Co-operation on a large scale requires a directing authority, provided by the capitalist. This authority has two aspects; it is a functional necessity, but it takes a 'despotic' form because of the inherently antagonistic relation between worker and capitalist. A new theme emerges here, one that Marx will develop in the following chapters. In a capitalist system, an increasing productivity of labour goes along with a progressive loss of freedom, at least within the labour process. The actual producers exercise less and less control over their own activities. Marx does not draw explicit political conclusions, but he thought, of course, that the overthrow of capitalism would reverse the trend.

Chapter 14. Division of labour and manufacture

Section 1. Two-fold origin of manufacture

By *manufacture* Marx means a form of co-operation in which different specialized workers (*detail labourers*) each carry out a particular operation by hand. (Marx's use of the term differs from that which is common now, in which manufacture is opposed to mining, agriculture, services, and so on.) The *manufacturing period*, in which manufacture (in Marx's sense) predominated, stretched from the mid-sixteenth to the late eighteenth centuries.

Manufacture arises in two ways. Crafts formerly carried out by independent craftsmen may be brought together, and their scope drastically limited, so that a locksmith, say, employed by a carriage maker only produces a certain type of carriage lock. Alternatively, a production process previously carried out by unspecialized workers may be subdivided into a series of specialized tasks, so that the production of locks, say, is divided into a succession of operations producing components and then assembling them.

Section 2. The detail labourer and his implements

The detail labourer carries out a single, specialized task, and perfects a limited manual skill to an extent that would otherwise be impossible. The time that would be lost in switching from one activity to another is saved. Specialized tools can be designed for each specific task; the subsequent development of machinery, which is the subject of the next chapter, starts from this subdivision of activities and tools.

Section 3. The two fundamental forms of manufacture

Heterogeneous manufacture is the production and subsequent assembly of a number of components, as in the manufacture of watches. Marx says little about this form. *Serial manufacture* involves successive processes carried out on the same materials, so that the work of each labourer provides raw materials for the next. Marx's examples are the manufacture of paper and of needles. There must be an appropriate distribution of workers between different tasks, and order and regularity must be maintained throughout to permit an even flow of work with no interruptions.

Machinery may be introduced into various stages of a process that is still carried out mainly by hand, but in the manufacturing period proper it played a subordinate role. Nevertheless, these early uses of machinery stimulated the science of mechanics in the seventeenth century and 'bequeathed to us the great inventions of the compass, of gunpowder, of type-printing and of the automatic clock' (p. 348).

The whole assembly of detail labourers makes up the *collective labourer*. Different workers have different individual skills, with 'a hierarchy of labour-powers, to which there corresponds a scale of wages' (p. 349). Overall, however, skills are reduced, since each worker possesses only a small fraction of the skill that would be needed to carry through the whole process. The cost of training is reduced, and with it the value of labour-power.

Section 4. Division of labour in manufacture and division of labour in society

The division of labour is a theme particularly associated with Adam Smith (though Marx shows both explicitly and implicitly, through his footnote quotations, that many of the key ideas predate Smith's writings). Smith lumped all forms of division of labour together, and approved of them all as ways of raising productivity. Marx is more sceptical about the benefits.

Historically, the division of labour has two starting points, which prefigure the two forms discussed below. Division of labour emerges first within the family, based on differences of age and sex. A quite different kind of division of labour originates in exchange, at first between separate communities, later within a single community. In a much quoted phrase, Marx remarks that: 'The foundation of every division of labour that is well developed, and brought about by the exchange of commodities, is the separation between town and country' (p. 352). The extent of a division of labour based on exchange depends on the density of population, the efficiency of transport and the development of production in general. Each extension of the division of labour, by creating demands for raw materials, specialized equipment, and so on, promotes its further extension.

Marx now introduces a crucial distinction between the *social division of labour* and the *division of labour in the workshop*. The social division of labour is that between independent producers of commodities. It entails a dispersion of ownership of means of production between many separate producing units, and is regulated by spontaneous market forces. The division of labour in the workshop differs from the social division of labour in every respect. Detail labourers do not produce separate commodities; ownership of the means of production is concentrated into the hands of a single capitalist; the process is under conscious central control. In a capitalist system, 'anarchy in the social division of labour and despotism in that of the workshop are mutual conditions the one of the other' (p. 356).

Marx contrasts this capitalist form of organization with other forms of the division of labour. His description of the Indian village community is particularly interesting, since his (few) writings on the 'Asiatic' mode of production have stimulated considerable debate. 'The simplicity of the organization for production in these self-sufficing communities . . . supplies the key to the secret of the unchangeableness of Asiatic societies' (p. 358).

Section 5. The capitalistic character of manufacture

The manufacturing division of labour can now be put into context as a stage in the development of capitalism.

A developed division of labour in the workshop requires relatively large units of production. If these are to be operated by capitalists, ownership of capital must be concentrated into larger units than those normally required for simple co-operation. It becomes harder still to become a capitalist.

Manufacture 'converts the labourer into a crippled monstrosity, by forcing his detail dexterity at the expense of a world of productive capabilities and instincts' (p. 360). *Manual* and *mental labour* are separated and turned into distinct specialisms. The worker is forced to sell his labour-power, not only because he cannot afford means of production, but also because his narrow skills can only function productively within an organization controlled by a capitalist. Working class resistance is not completely crushed. 'Since handicraft skill is the foundation of manufacture . . . capital is constantly compelled to wrestle with the insubordination of the workmen' (p. 367).

Chapter 15. Machinery and modern industry

The introduction of machinery marks the stage of *modern industry*. Marx's treatment of machinery has two main themes. Firstly, machinery displaces workers and, at the same time, makes it possible for women and children to be drawn into the labour force. The demand for labour-power is reduced, the supply enhanced, and the reserve army of the unemployed (which will be discussed in its own right later) is constantly renewed. The bargaining power of the workers is drastically reduced. Secondly, reinforcing this trend, mechanization completes the destruction of the independent skills of the worker and subjects him even more completely to the power of capital. Machinery, which could in principle lighten the burden of labour, serves instead to intensify it.

Section 1. The development of machinery

A machine 'supersedes the workman, who handles a single tool, by a mechanism operating with a number of similar tools, and set in motion by a single motive power' (p. 376). The tool is taken out of the hands of the worker, who no longer needs the specialized manual dexterity that characterized the manufacturing stage. The limits imposed by human capabilities no longer apply; 'the process as a whole is examined . . . without regard to the question of its execution by human hands . . . and the problem . . . is solved by the aid of machines, chemistry, etc.' (p. 380).

Marx distinguishes between the 'co-operation' of machines of the same kind operated by a single motive power (analogous to simple co-operation between human workers) and a system made out of a sequence of detail machines (analogous to the manufacturing division of labour among detail labourers), and builds up to a vision of 'a mechanical monster whose body fills whole factories, and whose demon power . . . at length breaks out into the fast and furious whirl of his countless working organs' (pp. 381–2).

Mechanization cannot be seen as a number of isolated 'inventions' in particular industries. 'A radical change . . . in one sphere of industry involves a similar change in other spheres' (p. 383). Major improvements at one stage of a process can only bear their full fruits if the other stages are correspondingly developed. Communications and transport must also be improved. The full benefits of mechanization cannot accrue until machines are themselves made by machines. The 'industrial revolution' (Marx does not use the term here, but he does elsewhere) is a single, interconnected process stretching down to Marx's own time. It is described with unmistakable admiration. Marx was not against technology or machines, but he was appalled by their effects in a capitalist system.

Section 2. The value transferred by machinery to the product

As usual, Marx has dealt first with the production of use-values, and now turns to the production of value and surplus-value. A durable machine transmits only a fraction of its value to each unit of the product. Machines may have a very high value by comparison with the simpler implements of earlier periods, but they are so productive that the value transferred to each unit of product, and hence the cost per unit, may be lower. The saving in direct labour is, however, even greater. The value of each unit of the product falls, and the ratio of means of production to labour-power, c/v, rises. The latter point will be developed at length later.

Marx next argues that the introduction of more mechanized techniques will reduce employment and put workers out of jobs, causing what is now called 'technological unemployment'. A machine will only be used if it saves on wage costs by displacing direct production workers. On the other hand, jobs will be created in the building of machines. Mechanization will be worthwhile (to the capitalist) if the saving on direct wage costs, over the life of the machine, outweighs its cost. All of the saving is on wage costs, but part of the value of the machine consists of surplus-value in machine building. (The machine using industry is assumed to pay for machines at their value.) It follows that more jobs are destroyed in the machine using industry than are created in machine building, for a given final output. (Accumulation and economic expansion counteract this by creating an extra demand for labour-power, which will be considered in part seven.)

The higher wages are, the more the incentive to use machines to displace direct labour. Where wages are low, machinery may not be used since low-wage direct labour is cheaper. Low wages do not cheapen machinery; they mean that there is more surplus-value in machine building.

Section 3. The proximate effects of machinery on the workmen

Most handicraft activities require a certain strength; minding a machine does not. Mechanization made it possible to employ women and children instead of (or as well as) adult male workers, drastically lowering the value of labour-power. The value of labour-power is determined by the commodities needed to reproduce the working class family. If more members of the family work, the costs of reproducing labour-power are spread over more workers, and each can be paid less. With lower wages, it becomes necessary for women and children to work to enable the family to survive.

Marx goes on to record the dreadful effects of the employment of women and children on family life, health, and so on. He is not against women and children working; in fact he thought that education for children should be combined with practical experience of productive work. He is against women and children (and men) being forced to suffer the conditions that then existed in capitalist factories.

The introduction of machinery led to a lengthening of the working-day, a paradoxical effect of labour-saving techniques. Capitalists want to use expensive machinery for as many hours per day as possible. Even if the machinery will wear out in half the time if used for twice the hours per day, the owner is anxious to get his profit before it is eroded by competition from still newer and better machines, an effect that Marx calls 'moral depreciation' (the modern term is 'obsolescence'). Capitalists can enforce longer hours, because the displacement of labour intensifies competition for jobs, while the employment of women and children breaks the resistance of traditional (male) craft organizations.

Once the working-day is shortened by law (see chapter ten), intensification of labour by speeding-up of machines and by making each worker supervise more machines takes its place. Intensification of work is equivalent to lengthening the day, since more actual labour is performed in the same time. Extraction of absolute surplus-value (more work) is superimposed on relative surplus-value (higher productivity).

Section 4. The factory

The mechanized factory can be seen in two ways, either as the 'co-operation of many orders of workpeople', or as a 'vast automaton . . . subordinate to a self-regulated moving force' (pp. 418–19; Marx quoting Ure). The first applies to the mechanized factory in general, the latter to machinery as used by capital. With this distinction Marx returns to another continuing theme: the progressive subordination of the worker that accompanies each increase in the productive power of labour.

Mechanization destroys the hierarchy of skills characteristic of manufacture, and reduces the great majority of workers to machine minders, factory operatives.

The destruction of skill is paralleled by a destruction of freedom. 'At the same time that factory work exhausts the nervous system to the uttermost, it does away with the many-sided play of the muscles, and confiscates every atom of freedom, both in bodily and intellectual activity . . . By means of its conversion into an automaton, the instrument of labour confronts the labourer . . . in the shape of capital, of dead labour, that dominates, and pumps dry, living labour-power. The separation of the intellectual powers of production from the manual labour . . . is . . . finally completed' (pp. 422–3). The indictment is completed by a brief reference to the appalling material conditions in factories, but Marx's attack is mounted primarily in the name of human freedom.

Section 5. The strife between workman and machine

There has been class conflict throughout the history of capitalism, but it was only with the introduction of machines that workers turned their anger against the instruments of production. Marx briefly reviews the history of machine-breaking (the Luddite movement, and so on) before turning to the reasons. In the manufacturing period labour was generally scarce, so productivity improvements did not usually threaten jobs. The introduction of machines, by contrast, caused unemployment, destroyed skills, and acted as a means of breaking workers' resistance to longer hours of work. It is not surprising that the workers reacted.

Section 6. The theory of compensation as regards the workpeople displaced by machinery

Some economists had answered criticisms of mechanization by arguing that any loss of jobs caused directly by machines would be offset by the creation of an equal number of jobs in other industries. The argument, in the form in which Marx takes it on, would not now be supported by anyone, but some important points emerge in Marx's critique. The main issue has already been dealt with; jobs are created in machine building, but fewer than are lost in machine using industries. It is true, as was argued by Marx's opponents, that the same amount of means of subsistence are available as before, but this is irrelevant, since workers who are unemployed have no wages with which to buy the means of subsistence.

In a growing economy, new jobs are constantly being created, but the point is that mechanization, by itself, reduces employment. The composition of employment also changes. The social division of labour is expanded, while the great increase in profits leads to a massive expansion of domestic service (a prominent feature of Victorian England) and of luxury industries catering to the tastes of the rich.

Section 7. Repulsion and attraction of workpeople by the factory system

Modern capitalism also creates insecurity. Skills are constantly being destroyed and industries undermined, while the cycle of boom and slump means that workers are constantly losing their jobs and then being re-employed. The industrial cycle is not explained here, but it is documented, in copious detail, as a fact of life.

Section 8. Revolution effected in manufacture, handicrafts and domestic industry by modern industry

Modern industry does not displace older forms overnight. By throwing people out of work, destroying skills and increasing insecurity, it tends to lengthen hours and drive down wages. Domestic and handicraft industries profit from these conditions. As particular stages of production are mechanized, new handicraft activities spring up and old activities expand to meet the needs of the greatly increased level of production, so handicrafts act, for a time, as a sort of auxiliary to the factory system. Domestic industries, those in which the work is done at home, are often the scene of even more appalling exploitation than is found in factories. Marx documents the dreadful conditions in these 'sweated' trades.

Marx is clearly aware of a sort of equilibrating mechanism at work, though he does not set it out explicitly. Mechanization drives down wages, and then the low wages serve to slow down the spread of mechanization by making handicrafts competitive. The Factory Acts, by limiting exploitation, accelerated mechanization.

Section 9. The Factory Acts. Sanitary and educational clauses of the same. Their general extension in England

The contents of section nine are pretty well summed up by its splendidly Victorian title. Its main interest is in the hints Marx gives, in the first few pages, of his ideas about education. After that, he documents a variety of exploitative and oppressive practices revealed by Select Committee enquiries.

Section 10. Modern industry and agriculture

The tantalizingly short final section of the chapter reverts to another of Marx's themes, the separation of town and country, which 'destroys at the same time the health of the town labourer and the intellectual life of the rural labourer' (p. 505). Marx calls for a 'union of agriculture and industry' without going into detail, and also charges capitalist agriculture with destroying the lasting sources of the fertility of the soil.

PART 5

Production of absolute and of relative surplus-value

Each of the first four parts of volume one represents a major advance in Marx's story. Part five is a sort of pause; Marx gathers the threads together, and completes a number of ideas that could not have been dealt with properly at an earlier stage.

Chapter 16. Absolute and relative surplus-value

In chapter seven, *productive labour* was considered simply as labour that produces use-values. Anyone who performs a necessary function in production is a part of the 'collective labourer', and is productive in this sense, even though there is no identifiable use-value produced by that specific individual. On the other hand, a labourer is only *productive for capital* if he produces surplus-value. Marx's example is a schoolteacher in a school run for profit. This example makes it clear that production of material objects is not the defining feature of productive labour in Marx's use of the term, although it was for Adam Smith. It is not clear why Marx should want to define productive labour, since he does not contrast it with unproductive labour, nor does he make much use of the concept later on.

He then explains that absolute and relative surplus-value can only be distinguished when we are concerned with *changes* in the rate of surplus-value.

The next topic is the natural basis of surplus-value. Unless natural conditions are such that workers can produce more than they need for subsistence, there can be no surplus-value. However, favourable natural conditions need not lead to exploitation at all, even less to specifically capitalist exploitation. The chapter concludes with criticisms of Ricardo and Mill for confusing the production of use-values with the production of surplus-value, and thus for ignoring the specific social relations that characterize capitalism.

Chapter 17. Changes of magnitude in the price of labour-power and in surplus-value

Marx now runs through some straightforward exercises in the application of his analysis, for the sake of completeness, or perhaps to ensure that the reader has been paying attention. He considers three variables: the length of the working-day, the intensity of labour and the productiveness of labour. An increase in the productiveness of labour reduces the value of labour-power and increases the rate of surplus-value (relative surplus-value). An increase in the intensity of labour or, equivalently, a lengthening of the working-day also increases the rate of surplus-value (absolute surplus-value). As Marx says, the consequences of simultaneous changes in two or three of these variables are easily worked out.

Chapter 18. Various formulae for the rate of surplus-value

The contents of chapter eighteen are indicated by its title. It introduces nothing new.

PART 6

Wages

Marx's analysis of surplus-value hinges on the distinction between labour and labour-power. The worker sells labour-power and is paid the value of his labour-power. What the capitalist gets from the worker is value-creating labour. In everyday life, however, no-one makes this distinction, and workers are paid *wages* either at an hourly rate or on a piece work basis. Marx must take account of these facts, which do not present him with much difficulty.

Chapter 19. The transformation of the value of labour-power into wages

The economists of Marx's time treated wages as the value of labour. Since value, in Marx's framework, is created by labour, he regards the 'value of labour' as an absurdity. If workers were paid for their labour, for the value they create, they would either be paid in full, leaving no surplus-value, or they would be paid less than the value created, which would apparently be a violation of the principle that value is exchanged for value. Either way, it would not be possible to explain capitalism in terms of the exchange of equal values. Marx gets around these problems by making a sharp distinction between the value of labour-power, which is what the worker sells, and the value created by labour. Where the classical economists arrived at correct results without making this distinction, they did so by investigating the value of labour-power, and simply calling it 'the value of labour'.

According to Marx, demand and supply cannot be used to

explain wages, since they only explain deviations from the 'necessary' or 'normal' price. Modern economists will blink at this statement; the point is that 'demand' and 'supply' were conceived, in Marx's time, in terms of deviations from normal levels of sales and output, and so could not be used to explain 'normal' conditions. The demand and supply analysis presented in modern textbooks is different; it does explain prices, and is not necessarily inconsistent with Marx's analysis.

The wage, Marx says, is merely the form in which payment for labour-power is made. The hourly wage is the value (or, strictly, price) of a day's labour-power divided by the normal number of hours worked per day. It is as if the price of a horse was quoted at so much per leg; multiply by four to find the price per horse. The price of labour-power is normally quoted at so much per hour.

It is not that anyone is trying to deceive in this way. In a commodity producing society there is no need to calculate the value of labour-power or of any other commodity. Sellers simply seek the highest price the market will bear, while buyers look for the best bargain. Prices are the unplanned outcome of this spontaneous bargaining. How market prices relate to values has yet to be explained. (See volume three, part two.) Here Marx is assuming that prices correspond to values.

Chapter 20. Time-wages

The determination of time-wages has already been explained. The hourly wage is the value of a day's labour-power divided by the number of hours in a normal working-day. A lengthening of the normal working-day therefore means a reduction of hourly wages, and so on. The actual price (wage) received may differ from the value of labour-power.

Chapter 21. Piece-wages

Wages are often paid by the piece produced instead of by the hour.

This gives the appearance that workers are selling their product, which is of course not so; the product does not belong to them, and they get the value of their labour-power, not the value of their product. The normal wage per piece is the daily value of labour-power divided by the number of pieces produced under average conditions in a working-day of normal length. Piece-work reduces, indeed eliminates, the need for superintendance, and is therefore appropriate to domestic industry and to the sub-letting (or sub-contracting) of labour. It helps to raise the intensity of labour, and is 'the form of wages most in harmony with the capitalist mode of production' (p. 556).

Chapter 22. National differences of wages

Marx's analysis of the factors that cause changes in the rate of surplus-value can also be used to examine differences between countries. Within a single country, the value of a product is determined by the labour required to produce it, with an average level of intensity and productiveness. Labour that is more intense or more productive produces more value. Similarly, on a world scale, an hour of 'normal' labour in a country where the 'normal' intensity or productiveness of labour is relatively high will produce more value than an hour of the 'normal' labour of other countries.

Marx has argued that the productiveness and intensity of labour rise as capital develops, so an hour of labour will create more value in an advanced than in a less advanced country. This may appear to contradict the general presumption that the values of commodities fall, as time goes by, rather than the value created by an hour of labour rising. The point is that goods produced in more advanced and less advanced countries must be sold on the same world-market at the same time. In this story, value is exchanged for value on the world-market and exchange is not unequal (there might be unequal exchange for other reasons, not dealt with here). If the product of an hour's labour in one country does not exchange for the product of an hour's labour in another, it is because they do not represent an equal amount of value. Some modern Marxists see matters differently.[5]

Wages, then (both in money and in buying power), may be higher in a more advanced country, while the rate of surplus-value may also be higher, since the value created by labour is so much greater. Except for the twist over international values, this is a simple application of the theory of relative surplus-value. The implication, incidentally, is that wages can, and generally do, rise as capitalism advances, which is not how some commentators interpret Marx.

PART 7

The accumulation of capital

Value and surplus-value have so far been analysed in terms of a single cycle of production, starting with money and ending with money ($M - C - M'$). The discussion of relative surplus-value did involve changes in the productiveness of labour, but in terms of 'snapshots' of a capitalist economy at various stages of development: co-operation, manufacture, modern industry. Now the time has come to look at *accumulation*, the actual growth of the scale of production from one period to the next. Marx starts with *simple reproduction*, repetition of production on an unchanged scale, in order to lay the groundwork.

He first sets out his assumptions. Commodities are assumed to be sold at their values without any holdups; the functions of exchange will be examined in more detail in volume two. The capitalist is assumed to keep all of the surplus-value produced; the division of surplus-value into various parts (interest, rent, etc.) will be dealt with in volume three.

Chapter 23. Simple reproduction

The short chapter on simple reproduction is one of the most important in *Capital*, and brings out very clearly Marx's view of capital as 'value in process, money in process' (p. 154, chapter four, quoted above).

Production is a continuous process; all the elements of production, material and social, must therefore be constantly renewed or *reproduced*. This renewal is often regarded as unproblematic by non-Marxist economists, but Marx stresses that means of production and labour-power are constantly (productively) consumed and must be constantly replaced. From the point of view of use-values, all the means of production which are used up must be replaced, so a part of output must consist of appropriate products, and must be reserved for that purpose. From the point of view of the capitalist production of value and surplus-value, capital must be reproduced as capital and advanced afresh.

If the capitalist consumes all of the surplus-value that he gets, and simply advances a capital of the same size in each period, then production continues at a constant level. This is what Marx calls *simple reproduction*. It is an analytical device to pick out those features of reproduction that arise out of simple continuity, before going on to look at reproduction on an ever-increasing scale.

Marx deals first with two features of capitalist production that may obscure the main points. Firstly, workers are paid in money. Looking at the whole system, however, the capitalist class pays wages ('order notes') to the workers, and the workers return these 'notes' to the capitalists in return for part (only a part) of their own produce. Secondly, to become a capitalist in the first place, the capitalist must have started with money derived from some previous source. (In part eight, Marx will examine the origins of capitalism and the capitalist class.) In any case, the capitalist must consume and if he received no surplus-value he would eventually consume all of his capital, so that continued capitalist production is possible only because surplus-value is produced; 'the mere continuity of the process of production . . . converts every capital into . . . capitalised surplus-value' (p. 570). This argument is directed against the 'abstinence' justification for profit, which will be discussed further in the next chapter.

The capitalist class starts with a certain capital, while the workers have nothing to sell but their labour-power. The wages paid in return for labour-power serve to reproduce the labour force (with all the necessary skills). Since workers get only just enough to meet their consumption needs, they end up as poor as before, and must offer their labour-power for sale again. The capitalist class have recouped their advances, plus surplus-value, and can thus consume the surplus-value and still have sufficient capital to start again, just as before. The material and social conditions for capitalist production and for the production of surplus-value have been reproduced.

'Capitalist production, therefore, under its aspect of a continuous connected process, of a process of reproduction, produces not only commodities, not only surplus-value, but it also produces and reproduces the capitalist relation; on the one side the capitalist, on the other the wage-labourer' (p. 578).

Chapter 24. Conversion of surplus-value into capital

Section 1. Capitalist production on a progressively increasing scale

A capitalist, instead of consuming surplus-value, can advance it as additional capital, so that his capital is larger in each successive period. This is *accumulation*, or *reproduction on a progressively increasing scale*, or *expanded reproduction* (Marx uses a variety of terms both here and later). In terms of values, it is a matter of simple arithmetic; capital to start with plus surplus accumulated equals capital in the next period.

In terms of use-values, recall the idea that the total product (of a complete, closed economy) can be divided in proportion to the components of its value; c, v and s (chapter nine, sections two and four). For the whole economy, the part corresponding to c, the used up means of production, must actually consist of means of production to replace those used up. The part corresponding to v, the value of labour-power, must consist of subsistence goods for the workers (Marx omits consideration of this part here; it was implicitly dealt with in chapter twenty-three). For simple reproduction, the part corresponding to s, the surplus product, consists of consumption goods for capitalists to consume. For accumulation to be possible it must instead consist of additional means of production and of subsistence, in appropriate proportions. There must also be additional labour-power available to be purchased. From the point of view of the working class as a whole, it is the products of one year's labour that confront it as extra capital in the following year.

Section 2. Erroneous conception, by political economy, of reproduction on a progressively increasing scale

Marx turns aside for a moment to clarify the relation between his theory and that of his predecessors. Smith and Ricardo correctly recognized that the part of surplus spent on employing extra productive workers (in addition to the number already employed) should be counted as accumulation, while employing unproductive workers (such as domestic servants) counts as consumption, and mere hoarding of money is neither. They went wrong, however, in assuming that accumulation consists entirely of advancing wages to additional workers, thus ignoring the additional means of production required to expand production. Incidentally, most modern economists go to the other extreme in assuming that capital is wholly accounted for by means of production.

Section 3. Separation of surplus-value into capital and revenue. The abstinence theory

The capitalist divides surplus-value between consumption and accumulation. As personified capital, he should expand his capital. (The rhetorical flourishes here do not make it clear why.) In addition, the pressures of competition force him to expand his capital. (Marx has emphasized throughout part four how efficiency requires larger and larger scales of operation as capitalism develops.) However, the temptations of luxury beckon and, to appear creditworthy, he must sustain a certain standard of consumption.

In the early stages of capitalism, Marx argues, the pressure to accumulate was the stronger. The famous exclamation 'Accumulate, accumulate! That is Moses and the prophets' (p. 595) is Marx's rendering of the attitude of the classical economists. The later 'vulgar' economists regarded accumulation as a subtraction from the capitalist's enjoyment of luxury, and justified profit on the grounds that it is a reward for 'abstinence'. In Marx's view, of course, it is the workers who are doing the abstaining.

Section 4. Circumstances that determine the amount of accumulation

Given the division of surplus-value between accumulation and consumption, the scale of accumulation clearly depends on the amount of surplus-value, which in turn is governed by factors already discussed. If wages can be forced down, or if labour becomes more intense or more productive, more accumulation is possible. As productivity goes up, the value of commodities falls, so the same amount of surplus-value will permit the capitalist to purchase more commodities, and as the number of workers grows, the same *rate* of surplus-value corresponds to an even greater *mass* of surplus-value. The capitalists' purchasing-power therefore constantly rises, allowing both luxury consumption and accumulation to increase.

Section 5. The so-called labour-fund

To round off the chapter, Marx returns to the attack on 'vulgar economy', this time attacking the labour-fund or wages-fund doctrine. The idea behind this (long obsolete) doctrine was that a fixed fund was available to pay wages. Some theorists argued that the level of wages was determined by dividing the fund between the (given) number of workers employed, while others explained employment by dividing the size of the fund by a fixed wage. In either case, according to Marx, they ignored all the important variables that determine the rate of accumulation. The description of Bentham, incidentally, both in the text and in the footnote, is a classic in the annals of invective.

Chapter 25. The general law of capitalist accumulation

Now that the concept of accumulation has been examined in isolation, in essentially quantitative terms, Marx can place it in a context of continuous technical revolution and look at the effects on the working class.

> *Section 1. The increased demand for labour-power that accompanies accumulation, the composition of capital remaining the same*

First, Marx establishes an essential set of concepts. The *value-composition of capital* is the ratio of constant to variable capital, c/v, measured, of course, in values. The *technical composition of capital* is its counterpart in terms of use-values, the mass of means of production relative to the living labour employed.

The technical composition cannot be measured quantitatively, since means of production and labour are qualitatively different things; one cannot be divided by the other. Therefore, Marx defines the *organic composition of capital*, which is the 'value-composition of capital, in so far as it is determined by its technical composition and mirrors the changes of the latter' (p. 612). Changes in the organic composition, in other words, show how the value-composition would have changed had the values of the individual commodities used as means of production, and the value of labour-power, remained constant. Economists today use similar procedures, for example in calculating national income 'at constant prices' i.e. removing the effects of inflation.

Suppose, for example, that a particular capital consists of 100 value units of constant capital and 50 value units of variable capital. Its value-composition is 2 ($c/v = 100/50 = 2$), and if we take this as our starting point, we can take the organic composition to be 2 as well (no change in the technical composition has yet occurred). Now suppose that a technical change leads to a 25 per cent increase in the means of production used, with a halving of labour-power employed. If the values of individual units of means of production and labour-power had stayed the same, c would have become 125, and v, 25, so the organic composition rises to 5 ($= 125/25$), which 'mirrors the change' in the technical composition of capital. At the same time, however, means of production may have been cheapened, so that c actually falls, say to 75, and the value-composition only rises to 3 (= 75/25). The organic composition is a measure of changes in the technical composition, and has to be measured from a given starting point.

The average composition of capital is the composition (value or organic, according to context) of the total social capital of a country. Where the composition of capital is mentioned without qualification, the organic composition should normally be understood, unless the context suggests otherwise. Marx is not always clear about which measure of the composition of capital he is using.

If accumulation takes place with no technical change, and hence with all three measures of the composition of capital remaining constant, there will be an equal proportional increase in constant and variable capital, and therefore in the demand for labour-power. This must (Marx says) ultimately outstrip the growth of the labouring population, so the demand for labour will exceed the supply and wages will rise.

At best, however, an increase in wages lessens the burden of exploitation; it cannot, while capitalism persists, end it. A lessening of exploitation means less surplus-value to accumulate, a slackening of the demand for labour-power and an end to the increase in wages. The needs of accumulation therefore set an upper limit to the level of wages as long as capitalism survives. As accumulation varies over the industrial cycle, so wages rise and fall. 'To put it mathematically: the rate of accumulation is the independent, not the dependent, variable; the rate of wages the dependent, not the independent, variable' (p. 620). Marx's account of wage movements is the opposite of the story told by some Marxists, for whom low (not high) wages threaten accumulation by restricting markets. At this stage, of course, Marx is explicitly ignoring any problem in selling the product.

Section 2. Relative diminution of the variable part of capital simultaneously with the progress of accumulation and of the concentration that accompanies it

So far, the composition of capital has been held constant. However, as the productivity of labour rises, so does the technical and hence the organic composition of capital. The materials worked by each labourer increase in volume, and so does the equipment he operates. The value of a given amount of the means of production will, of course, fall, which offsets the rise in the technical composition of capital. Nevertheless, Marx asserts, the value-composition of capital rises, albeit more slowly than the organic composition (which mirrors the technical composition). This assertion is regarded as self-evident and is not supported by any evidence; it is merely illustrated by some perfunctory numerical examples. The trend of the value-composition becomes of great importance in volume three, in connection with the falling rate of profit, and has been the subject of much debate. We can also note that productivity increases which reduce the value of means of production will devalue existing capital; this is not taken into account in the argument that follows.

As accumulation proceeds, individual capitals grow. Growth of units of capital by simple accumulation of surplus-value is called *concentration of capital*, which is 'only another name for reproduction on an extended scale' (p. 627). (Marx's use of the phrase differs from that in modern non-Marxist economics, in which 'concentration' refers to the size of firms relative to the size of an industry.) *Centralization of capital*, by contrast, refers to the regrouping of existing capital into fewer units, through takeovers, mergers or the buying-up of the assets of bankrupt firms. Competition promotes centralization, since large capitals have lower costs and drive out smaller ones. Small capitals are forced into backward branches of the economy where they are massacred by intense competition. The credit system channels control over capital to larger enterprises, as does the development of the joint-stock form of organization. Accumulation, then, promotes concentration and centralization, which in turn promote increased efficiency, raise the productivity of labour and increase the rate of surplus-value, accelerating accumulation even further. Along with all this, the organic composition of capital rises.

Section 3. Progressive production of a relative surplus-population or industrial reserve army

As the composition of capital rises, the demand for labour-power falls relatively, since a larger part of capital goes to buy means of production, and less to employ workers. 'The labouring population therefore produces . . . the means by which itself is made relatively superfluous, is turned into a relative surplus-population; and it does this to an always increasing extent' (p. 631).

This is a crucial step in Marx's argument, since it is the presence of the relative surplus-population that holds wages (the price of labour-power) down to the value of labour-power. Two main comments can be made. Firstly, what is relevant is the value-composition of capital, which determines the proportions in which capital is divided into constant and variable capital, though Marx only mentions the organic composition. Secondly, there are three factors at work: the increasing composition of capital (which, as noted, reduces the demand for labour-power), the accumulation of capital (which, by itself, increases the demand), and the growth in the size of the working class, determined by demographic and social factors (which increases the supply of labour-power). In predicting an *ever-increasing* relative surplus-population, Marx is clearly making a judgement about the relative strength of these factors; it is not clear that one can legitimately make that judgement on *a priori* grounds alone.

An *industrial reserve army* or *relative surplus-population*, that is, a mass of unemployed labour-power, is essential to capitalism, according to Marx. 'The mass of social wealth . . . thrusts itself frantically into old branches of production, whose market suddenly expands, or into newly formed branches . . . In all such cases there must be the possibility of throwing great masses of men suddenly on the decisive points . . . Over-population supplies these masses' (p. 632). The population is not, of course, excessive in any absolute sense, only relative to the employment that capital provides. Indeed, the working-day is lengthened and the intensity of work stepped-up. 'The condemnation of one part of the working-class to enforced idleness by the over-work of the other part, and the converse, becomes a means of enriching the individual capitalists, and accelerates at the same time the production of the industrial reserve army' (p. 636).

To finish the section, Marx deals with opposing theories. He ridicules Malthusian demographic explanations of wages and population, in which high wages raise birth rates and hence the supply of labour-power, on the grounds that the industrial cycle only lasts seven to ten years in total, while demographic reactions take much longer. He also repeats his criticisms of the theory of 'compensation', already dealt with in chapter fifteen, section six.

Section 5. Different forms of the relative surplus-population. The general law of capitalist accumulation

The reserve army of labour can be divided into different parts. The *floating* surplus-population consists of unemployed workers who have previously worked for capital and who are already in the industrial centres. They include men employed as juveniles and rejected once they reach maturity (and become more expensive), and those whose health has been ruined. This part of the reserve army is the most readily available to capital when it is needed. The industrial cycle alternately throws great masses of workers into the reserve army, and then draws them into employment again.

In rural areas, the development of capitalist agriculture has created massive underemployment (and corresponding low wages). This rural reserve army, which Marx calls the *latent surplus-population*, ensures that new workers for urban industry are always available.

The *stagnant reserve army* consists of those who are employed very rarely and irregularly, and who get very low wages when they are employed. They provide the labour force for 'sweated' handicrafts and domestic industry. At the lowest level are masses of paupers reduced to desperate poverty.

The '*absolute general law of capitalist accumulation*' says that 'The greater the social wealth . . . the greater is the industrial reserve army . . . The more extensive . . . the industrial reserve army, the greater is official pauperism' (p. 644). The impact of this striking conclusion is rather lessened by the addition: 'Like all other laws it is modified in its working by many circumstances, the analysis of which does not concern us here' (p. 644).

The pressure of competition for jobs not only keeps wages down, but also gives the capitalist the bargaining power to lengthen the working-day and intensify labour. Marx also reminds us of the destructive effects of mechanization on freedom and on working conditions. He comes, then, to the conclusion that 'in proportion as capital accumulates, the lot of the labourer, be his payment high or low, must grow worse' (p. 645).

Section 5. *Illustrations of the general law of capitalist accumulation*

In the final section of the chapter, as its title suggests, Marx presents a number of cases to back up the conclusions quoted above.

PART 8

The so-called primitive accumulation

Chapter 26. The secret of primitive accumulation

Marx has analysed capitalism as a self-reproducing system; once in existence it reproduces itself on an ever-increasing scale. He still has to explain how capital came into existence in the first place. *Primitive accumulation* is the original accumulation of capital before there was surplus-value, since surplus-value cannot be generated without capital to start with.

After a passing swipe at explanations in terms of the virtuous thrift of capitalists (or their ancestors), Marx sets up the problem. Money and commodities are not capital; to be transformed into capital they require the separation of the population into two classes, capitalists on the one hand, free workers on the other. 'The process therefore . . . takes away from the labourer the possession of his means of production . . . transforms, on the one hand, the social means of subsistence and of production into capital, on the other, the immediate producers into wage-labourers' (p. 714). Note that it is not a matter of augmenting the means of production (there is always a temptation to read 'accumulation' in this sense) but of transforming them *into capital*.

Capitalism developed out of feudalism, so primitive accumulation had two aspects. To produce workers 'free in the double sense' of being free individuals, but also 'free' of any ownership of means of production, involved firstly the emancipation of the producers, the breakdown of serfdom, of guild regulations, and so on, and secondly the expropriation of the producers, the separation of the producers from the means of production. Since 'the capitalistic era dates from the 16th century' (p. 715) and serfdom had long been abolished by that time in the areas that became the main centres of capitalist development, Marx focusses all his attention on the expropriation of the producers. His example is England, the first fully capitalist nation.

Chapter 27. Expropriation of the agricultural population from the land

England, around 1400, was mainly a nation of free peasant proprietors, owning and cultivating their land. Towns were prosperous and wage-labour played a subordinate role. The general standard of living was quite high (in his discussion of the working-day, Marx has already shown that it took centuries to extend hours of work to nineteenth-century levels). The centrepiece of primitive accumulation is the expulsion of this peasantry, and its conversion into a proletariat. The footnote reference to Japan as an example of feudalism is interesting, since Japan has since become the only country outside Europe, and areas of European settlement, to become a major capitalist power.

The process started in about 1500. Arable land was converted into sheep-walks, and the cultivators were expelled. The Flemish demand for wool was the main initiating factor here. (It seems a somewhat accidental and external factor to have started such an epoch making process.) Contributory factors included the effects of the Reformation, which broke up church holdings of land, and the end of the Wars of the Roses, which had provided employment for bands of mercenary soldiers, feudal retainers, and so on. At this early stage, the state generally resisted enclosures, while also repressing any resistance by the victims.

Even in the seventeenth century the 'yeomanry', the prosperous peasantry, was more numerous than the 'farmers'. (Note that Marx, here and elsewhere, means *capitalist* farmers, i.e. employers of wage-labour.) After the revolutions of the seventeenth century, the state switched sides, and started positively to encourage the enclosure of common lands and the expulsion of peasants. The final act, still being played out in Marx's own time, was the 'clearance' of estates in the Highlands of Scotland. By that time the independent peasantry was not even a memory in England. Capitalist agriculture had been established, and a 'free' proletariat created for urban industry.

Chapter 28. Bloody legislation against the expropriated

In the first stages of primitive accumulation, the proletariat was created faster than it could be absorbed into wage-labour, producing a mass of hapless vagabonds. Legislative action tried to reverse the process by punishing the victims, an act of apparently pointless sadism.

The general pattern of repression directed against the nascent working class had its purpose, however. In an established capitalist system the working class, seeing no alternative, is kept in its place by 'the dull compulsion of economic relations'. At the beginnings of capitalism, by contrast, the workers had to be tamed by force. Wage-labour was still scarce, wages high and profits low. A whole succession of laws were enacted that aimed (initially with little success) to force down wages and to outlaw trade unions (cf. legislation to extend the working-day, covered in chapter ten). The English parliament 'for 500 years, held . . . the position of a permanent Trades' Union of the capitalists against the labourers' (p. 741).

Chapter 29. Genesis of the capitalist farmer

Marx's main subject is the origin of capital, not the capitalist. However, the expropriation of the peasants transferred land to large landlords, while the system that emerged in agriculture involved three classes: landlords, tenant farmers (capitalist farmers), and wage-labourers. Where, then, did the tenant farmers come from? Originally, Marx says, the tenant farmer appeared in the fifteenth century as a marginally more successful peasant or as a bailiff. In the sixteenth century, prices rose, so that wages and rents both fell, in real terms, where they were fixed by agreement or by custom in terms of money. The result was a period of exceptional profits for the farmers, who emerged during that century as a distinct and important class.

Chapter 30. Reaction of the agricultural revolution on industry. Creation of the home-market

The creation of a proletariat is the precondition for the emergence of capitalism, so Marx's analysis of primitive accumulation starts with agriculture, with the expulsion of the peasantry. The origins of capitalist industry are part of the same story. In pre-capitalist England, most non-agricultural production was carried out in conjunction with agriculture, in rural domestic industries. The expulsion of the peasants from the land had several linked effects. Firstly, rural domestic industries were disrupted, creating a gap for the products of capitalist industry to fill, and at the same time making agricultural raw materials, which would previously have been processed locally, available for sale. The expelled peasants provided a labour-force for industry, while those who stayed on the land as agricultural labourers now had to work full time in agriculture, for extended hours and more intensively, supplying a surplus of agricultural produce to feed the new urban working class.

In principle a market could be created without any change in the volume of use-values produced at all, simply by forcing onto the market products that would not previously have been sold, and correspondingly forcing those who use the products to buy them in the market. Activities previously carried out within a single household or local community are now performed by distinct capitalist enterprises whose products are exchanged in the market. What has changed is the social relations of production. In practice, as Marx says, there was a concurrent technical revolution in agriculture.

Chapter 31. Genesis of the industrial capitalist

Along with the gradual transformation of agriculture into capitalist agriculture and the creation of a home-market, small artisans could, and did, become capitalists. Historically, however, this was not the main route by which the industrial capitalist class emerged, since the creation of a home-market was overshadowed by the opening up of the world-market.

Before capitalist production proper got under way, capital already existed in the form of usurer's capital and merchant's capital (which will be discussed further in volume three), but the nascent capitalists were barred from control of production by the feudal organization of agriculture and by the urban guilds. As restrictions on capitalist production broke down, these forms of capital could be transformed into industrial capital.

The question of the genesis of the industrial capitalist seems to be settled, but Marx now branches out into a discussion of the role of capitalist conquest outside Europe, a topic that has generated much debate among Marxists. The question is whether external sources of profit were the main cause of capitalist development in Europe, or whether they simply accelerated a process that was happening anyway. Since external conquest appears almost as an afterthought in Marx's argument, and since his main stress is on the creation of a proletariat inside England, it seems that Marx must have regarded external profits as a secondary factor. On the other hand, he comments that: 'These idyllic proceedings [looting, slavery, etc.] are the chief momenta of primitive accumulation' (p. 751). This and similar quotations are often cited by modern Marxists who want to argue that the impoverishment and exploitation of the 'Third World' was the direct cause of the rise of capitalism in Europe. A full assessment of Marx's views would require an examination of other comments in *Capital* (see, especially, chapter twenty of volume three) and of his other writings. Establishing what Marx thought on the question would not, of course, settle the question of fact.

Marx gives a very brief description of the system that arose in England at the end of the seventeenth century: 'a systematical combination embracing the colonies, the national debt, the modern mode of taxation, and the protectionist system. These methods . . . all employ the power of the state . . . Force is the midwife of every old society pregnant with a new one' (p. 751). Note that his emphasis is on the use of state power both internally and externally, and not only on external conquest.

He proceeds to give some rather randomly chosen examples of how this transitional system worked. He documents both the barbarities and the profitability of colonial conquest, and explains how public credit accelerated the development of financial institutions, while the taxes imposed to pay the interest on the national debt impoverished small producers and contributed to the formation of a proletariat. The cotton industry got its labour force by the conscription of pauper children, and its raw materials from the slave plantations of the United States. Capital, Marx concludes, comes into the world 'dripping from head to foot, from every pore, with blood and dirt' (p. 760).

Chapter 32. Historical tendency of capitalist accumulation

Marx now reaches his peroration (chapter thirty-three, which follows, is more of an appendix). In these few, much quoted, pages, he finally puts together his guiding vision of the past and future of capitalism. They are pages that should be read and savoured.

We start from the *petty mode of production*, which is production by individual, independent producers (peasants or artisans) who own their own means of production. This mode, incidentally, is interesting in that it does not appear in the conventional sequence of modes (primitive-communal, ancient, feudal, capitalist; see, for example, Marx's Preface to a *Contribution to the Critique of Political Economy*), and does not involve any class opposition or exploitation. 'It is compatible only with a system of production, and a society, moving within narrow and more or less primitive bounds' (p. 762).

'At a certain stage of development it brings forth the material agencies for its own dissolution' (p. 762). The individual producers are expropriated, and reduced to propertyless proletarians. Next, competition between capitalists expropriates the weaker, and concentrates production into even larger units. 'Along with the constantly diminishing number of magnates of capital . . . grows the mass of misery, oppression, slavery, degradation, exploitation; but with this too grows the revolt of the working class, a class always increasing in numbers, and disciplined, united, organised by the very mechanism of the process of capitalist production itself . . . The knell of capitalist private property sounds. The expropriators are expropriated' (p. 763).

Chapter 33. The modern theory of colonization

Marx ends volume one on an ironic note with a discussion of colonization built around the story of Mr Peel. Colonization, here, means occupation of empty lands, or lands from which the natives have been driven out, and does not refer to the exploitation of native populations. Mr Peel went to Australia provided with workers, with means of production, and with everything a capitalist might want. The only point he had overlooked was the need to keep his workers separated from the means of production in order that they should remain wage-workers; in other words, he ignored the central point that Marx has been making throughout *Capital*. Finding land freely available, all his workers abandoned the unfortunate Mr Peel 'who provided for everything except the export of English modes of production to Swan River!' (p. 766).

The process of circulation of capital

PART 1

The metamorphoses of capital and their circuits

The first volume of *Capital* is about the source of surplus-value. Once Marx has shown that surplus-value originates in production he relegates exchange to the background. In the second volume the focus shifts back to exchange, while still keeping the assumption that commodities exchange at their values. Competition, market prices, credit, interest and rent are left to be dealt with in volume three, so the analysis is still very abstract.

The second and third volumes of *Capital* were left unfinished when Marx died, and were put together by Engels from a rather confused mass of manuscripts. As a result, there is much more repetition than there is in volume one, and there are also inconsistencies and unfinished arguments.

There are three main ideas in the first part of volume two. Firstly, the reproduction of an individual capital involves a repeated alternation between the 'spheres' of production and of exchange. Means of production and labour-power are bought (in the sphere of exchange), commodities are produced (in the sphere of production) and sold for money (in the sphere of exchange), which is available to start the process again.

Secondly, the 'circuits' of different individual capitals are intertwined with each other. The means of production bought by one capitalist are the product of another. Workers are paid wages by one capitalist, and spend them on the products of other capitalists.

Thirdly, the system is vulnerable to 'crisis' because of the interdependence of different capitals. This is not a purely theoretical point; cyclical crises occurred every seven to ten years in the period in which Marx wrote. If demand falters, capitalists will be unable to sell their product, and will cut back on their purchases of means of production, and lay off workers. Demand will be reduced further, and the problem will be intensified. Marx has much to say about various aspects of the cyclical process, and especially about crises, but he never put together a complete, systematic theory of cycles.

Chapter 1. The circuit of money-capital

The concept of capital was first introduced (in volume one, part two) in terms of the formula $M - C - M'$. The capitalist advances money (M) to buy commodities (C), which are resold for more money (M'). Marx has argued that surplus-value is created in production, so he rewrites the formula as:

$$M - C \ldots P \ldots C' - M',$$

where $C \ldots P \ldots C'$ represent a production process that transforms one set of commodities (C) into another of greater value (C'). The dots around P show that it is an interruption in the sequence of exchange transactions. The two exchanges, $M - C$ and $C' - M'$, are exchanges of value for value.

The whole *circuit* or *circular movement* defines capital, which is not a thing but a process. None of the component parts of the process, taken by itself, is inherently capitalist. Production takes place in any society, capitalist or not, and exchanges take place in any commodity producing system.

Section 1. First stage. $M - C$

In itself $M - C$ is simply a purchase of commodities. The capitalist, however, does not buy commodities at random. He buys labour-power and means of production (in the appropriate proportions); this identifies the exchange as a stage in the circuit of capital, and the money laid out as *money-capital*. Marx therefore rewrites the circuit as:

$$M - C \begin{cases} L \\ MP \end{cases} \ldots P \ldots C' - M',$$

where *L* and *MP* stand for labour-power and means of production. Together they constitute *productive capital*.

The purchase of labour-power, $M - L$, defines a particular kind of class relation between the owners of the means of production and a class of free labourers. This relation makes it possible to transform money into capital, just as money can only buy slaves in a society in which the institution of slavery exists. Money is not inherently capital; it becomes capital only in a particular social context, and only as a stage in the circuit of capital.

Section 2. Second stage. Function of productive capital

There is little to say about production that has not already been said in volume one. To produce surplus-value, the capitalist must, of course, set labour-power to work to produce commodities.

The development of capitalist production makes the production of commodities universal. Workers must spend their wages on commodities. Capitalists must buy means of production which must therefore be for sale, must be produced in sufficient quantity as commodities.

Means of production may, however, be bought from non-capitalist (commodity) producers. 'Such was for instance the first effect of capitalist world commerce on such nations as the Chinese, Indians, Arabs, etc. But, secondly, wherever it takes root capitalist production destroys all forms of commodity production which are based either on the self-employment of the producers, or merely on the sale of the excess product' (p. 34).

Section 3. Third stage. $C' - M'$

The completed commodities embodying surplus-value are called *commodity-capital*. They must next be sold. Money-capital has been transformed first into productive capital, then into commodity-capital, and now, finally, into (augmented) money-capital; these are the 'metamorphoses' of capital referred to in the title of this part of the volume. Each form qualifies as capital by its role in the circuit as a whole. Nothing in the sale (*realization*) of commodity-capital identifies it as capital; the sale in itself is simply a sale of commodities at their value.

Section 4. The circuit as a whole

'Capital . . . appears as a value that goes through a series of interconnected, interdependent transformations . . . which form just as many phases, or stages, of the process as a whole' (pp. 47–8). Capital which goes through these stages is called *industrial capital*, the basic form of capital.

The circuit may be interrupted for many reasons. If so, unused money-capital may remain as a mere hoard, unused productive capital may show up as idle means of production and unemployed workers, or unsold commodities may clog the market.

In the normal course of events, without any unusual interruption, the process takes time. The turnover time of capital will be discussed in detail in volume two, part two.

Transport is a special case. Its useful effect is to change the location of something, and this effect cannot be stored before sale. There is no stage of commodity-capital awaiting sale in the case of transport. The useful effect of transport can, however, be thought of as a commodity; it can be consumed individually (e.g. a pleasure cruise) or productively (when means of production are transported). Labour expended in transport creates value.

Money-capital and commodity-capital can exist separately as 'vehicles of particular branches of business', but are subordinate to industrial capital, an observation that will be developed in detail in volume three, part four. Banks, merchants, and so on, may take over certain functions of industrial capital and receive a share of surplus-value, but surplus-value originates in production.

Finally, Marx points out that the reproduction of capital involves the continual repetition of the circuit, $M - C \ldots P \ldots C' - M' - C \ldots P \ldots C' - M'$, etc. The circuit does not really start anywhere, but could equally be thought of as starting with P (the viewpoint of the next chapter) or with C' (chapter three).

Chapter 2. The circuit of productive capital

Starting from P, the circuit appears as $P \ldots C' - M' - C \ldots P$. From this angle, circulation appears as a (necessary) periodic interruption of a constantly renewed production process.

Section 1. Simple reproduction

Simple reproduction is the (artificial) case in which the whole of surplus-value is spent on individual consumption by the capitalist, so that production is renewed on the same scale as before (assuming that all conditions remain unchanged). Whenever he deals with reproduction, Marx's standard procedure is to start with simple reproduction and then move on to consider accumulation.

Exchange now appears in the form $C - M - C$, just as in simple commodity circulation (volume one, chapter three). The aim of the capitalist, just like a simple commodity producer, seems to be merely the reconstitution of production, plus private consumption. Marx stresses that the capitalist's consumption comes out of surplus-value, and is therefore quite different from the consumption of a petty commodity producer, who consumes the value created by his own labour.

In the circuit of productive capital, money-capital plays only a transient role. It is the result of capitalist production (not the starting point, as it was in the previous chapter), and it is reconverted into productive capital and into commodities for the capitalist's consumption.

Once goods are sold, the individual capitalist need not worry about their future. If the general circulation of commodities is disrupted, individual capitalists may continue to sell their products for a while, as they pile up in the hands of wholesalers and merchants, but eventually production will be interrupted.

Section 2. Accumulation and reproduction on an extended scale

Surplus-value is not normally all spent on individual consumption;

part is accumulated. Since there is a minimum scale of new investment (varying in different branches of industry), surplus-value must
be hoarded as 'latent' money-capital until a large enough sum has
been collected.

Accumulation can be represented by the formula $P \ldots P'$; a productive capital, P, yields surplus-value which is accumulated, so
that the next cycle takes place on a larger scale, represented by P'.
Where $M \ldots M'$ represents a single cycle of production, yielding
surplus-value, $P \ldots P'$ represents accumulation.

Section 3. Accumulation of money

As already noted, surplus-value must be accumulated as money
before it can be transformed into additional productive capital.
Throughout volume two, one of Marx's concerns is with the normal
'rhythm' of production and exchange, and with potential interruptions in that rhythm, one of which is the accumulation of hoards of
money. At a later stage he will discuss how banks can mobilize
unused money to serve as active money-capital.

Section 4. Reserve fund

Latent money-capital (hoarded money waiting to be used as capital)
can serve as a reserve fund and permit continued production if, for
any reason, the sale of commodities is delayed.

As a closing comment on the chapter, Marx remarks that the
circuit of productive capital, the reproduction or reconstitution of
production from one period to the next, was the focus of attention
of classical political economy. Marx himself started from the
$M \ldots M'$ form of the circuit because it brings out the process of producing surplus-value more clearly.

Chapter 3. The circuit of commodity capital

The circular movement of capital can also be analysed starting from
C', the product of one cycle of production and ending with the

product of the next cycle. In terms of the whole social capital, the product is distributed between different uses, and is reproduced again in the next cycle. This was the point of view of Quesnay and the physiocrats.

The commodity-capital, C', must already be in the appropriate material form (means of production, articles designed for individual consumption, etc.) if reproduction is to be possible. The necessary relations of proportionality between different branches of production will be dealt with in part three of this volume.

Chapter 4. The three formulas of the circuit

The three formulas discussed in the first three chapters describe the same process from different angles. In a functioning economy, each presupposes the other, and different capitals pass through each phase in turn. At any time there are quantities of money and of finished goods on hand, there are production processes going on, and so on. Each capital is dependent on others, as suppliers and as customers. 'The industrial capital, continuously progressing along its orbit, thus exists simultaneously at all its stages and in the diverse functional forms corresponding to these stages' (p. 102).

The magnitude of the total social capital determines the overall scale of production. At any date, the size of the total capital is the result of previous stages of accumulation; it grows as accumulation proceeds. The functional needs of the process determine the division of the total capital between hoards of money, productive capital and commodity-capital. Interruption of any part of the process, if severe enough, can disrupt the whole and precipitate a crisis.

Normally, the commodities bought and sold in the circulation stages of the circuit are exchanged within the capitalist system, either in exchanges between capitalists, or between capitalists and workers. This need not always be so. Once a commodity is on the market its origin is immaterial, and it may be the product of non-capitalist producers. Capitalism, however, tends to undermine other modes of production, and to transform all direct producers into wage-workers. In the meantime, the products of non-capitalist modes normally pass through the hands of merchants who act (among their other functions) as intermediaries between industrial capital and other modes of production (see volume three, chapter twenty).

The chapter concludes with an incomplete discussion of the demand for commodities. In his role as capitalist, the capitalist supplies goods of greater value than those that he purchases (demands). Let the value of the product be $c + v + s$ (in the usual notation). The capitalist buys means of production with a value of c, and pays wages of v which the workers spend. It seems that demand only amounts to $c + v$, while supply is $c + v + s$; the difference, of course, is surplus-value.

In simple reproduction the capitalist spends the surplus-value, s, on individual consumption, so his total spending, plus that of the workers he employs, corresponds to the amount he has to sell. If this is so for all capitalists, total supply will match total demand.

In practice, however, capitalists accumulate. If they were to spend all of their surplus-value immediately, partly on individual consumption, partly on additional means of production and labour-power, total demand would still match total supply, since additional purchases of labour-power are translated into demand for produced goods when the extra workers spend their wages. The demand for particular commodities would be different from that in simple reproduction; more means of production and subsistence goods would be required, and fewer luxuries. The make-up of output would have to be different.

If surplus-value is hoarded as money while sufficient amounts are gathered to carry out viable investment projects, then a deficiency of demand will exist, threatening reproduction. Marx does not continue (the point will be taken up again later), but it is clear that undisturbed reproduction can continue if spending from previously accumulated hoards matches current hoarding (see chapters seventeen, twenty and twenty-one in this volume).

Chapter 5. The time of circulation

This chapter, on the time of circulation, overlaps to some extent with chapter twelve, which has the same title. They are taken from different (unfinished) manuscripts.

The duration of a complete cycle or turnover of capital consists of the time of production plus the time of circulation. Surplus-value is only created while labour is actually being performed, during the time of the labour-process. The time of production is longer than this, both because of interruptions of production (overnight, for example) and because of technically necessary intervals (in some cases), for example while wine matures or crops grow. Durable instruments of production turn over their value even more slowly, a fact that will be discussed more fully in the next part.

The time of circulation, in which capital is tied up as money-capital or commodity-capital, increases the length of the cycle further. Use-values may deteriorate with time, causing a loss of value if the circulation time is prolonged beyond its normal length. There are also costs of circulation (see the next chapter). No value or surplus-value is created during these stages of the cycle.

A given capital, in a given time, will produce less surplus-value if it is immobilized for a greater part of the time in circulation, where it produces no surplus-value. Political economy has been deceived by the calculation of profit as a percentage rate per year (or whatever), into thinking that the mere passage of time yields profit (surplus-value). As Marx will show later (volume three, part two) the equalization of profit rates between sectors of the economy adds colour to this belief.

Chapter 6. The costs of circulation

There are costs involved in trading in commodities. Marx's rule is that labour expended in circulation is not necessary for the production of use-values, and therefore creates no value. Costs incurred in buying and selling are a deduction from the capital available to produce surplus-value.

This ruling is, incidentally, of secondary importance. Suppose we were to break with Marx and count labour expended in circulation as productive of value. The value of commodities so defined would be higher, but so would the value of labour-power, since the commodities required by workers would be counted as having greater value. The real surplus-product available to the capitalist class after allowing for all costs would not be altered by the different method of computing values.

Section 1. Genuine costs of circulation

Time and labour are required for buying and selling. These activities may be carried out by the capitalist himself, or by employed workers, whose wages absorb part of variable capital without producing any value, or by merchants. Similarly, book-keeping is necessary. Part of social capital is tied up in money, in quantities of gold which cost labour to produce. These are the 'faux frais' (costs, burdens) of capitalist commodity production.

Section 2. Costs of storage

A mass of commodities must always exist in the market to 'form a supply', in other words to be available for purchase when required. Storage costs are incurred, in direct labour (watchmen, etc.) and in warehouses, and so on. In any society, stocks of means of production and of consumer goods must be held; in a capitalist commodity producing system they constitute a commodity-supply. The advance of capitalism expands the commodity-supply by converting stocks that were not commodities, because they were not for sale, into stocks of commodities. At the same time, stocks may be reduced (proportionately) by improvements in transport and communications, so that supplies arrive more regularly and frequently.

Section 3. Costs of transportation

Transportation, unlike simple purchase or sale, creates value, because it counts as a transformation of use-values. Progress in the transport industry reduces the labour required, and thus the value added by transport, just as advances in any other industry reduce the value of its product.

PART 2

The turnover of capital

Capitalist production of surplus-value is a circular process; money is advanced to buy labour-power and means of production, commodities are produced and sold for money, which is laid out again to continue the process. The rate of surplus-value measures the ratio of the surplus-value produced in a single cycle to the variable capital advanced. Marx now discusses the length of time taken by a cycle or turnover of capital. If the cycle is completed quickly, a given variable capital can generate more surplus-value in any given length of time, by completing more cycles of production, than it would if the cycle took longer. Matters are complicated by the existence of durable instruments of production (fixed capital) which require a large capital outlay and yield up their value slowly, and also by the possibility that capital may be advanced in stages during a lengthy production process.

Chapter 7. The turnover time and the number of turnovers

The *turnover time* is the time taken for one complete circuit or circular movement of capital; $M \ldots M'$, $P \ldots P$, or $C \ldots C$. The number of complete turnovers in a period T (say a year) is T/t, where t is the turnover time. If the turnover time is three months, for example, there are four $(12 \div 3)$ turnovers per year.

Chapter 8. Fixed and circulating capital

Section 1. Distinctions of form

Instruments of labour (tools, machines) are not used up in a single process of production, but last a period of time. Their value is transferred to the product in stages, over their normal lives. Marx calls the part of capital that is embodied in (durable) instruments of production, *fixed capital*. The remainder of constant capital (materials, fuels, etc.), together with variable capital (labour-power) is used up in a single cycle of production, and is called *circulating capital*.

Fixed capital is defined by the fact that its whole value is not transferred immediately to the product. Fertilizers that have a lasting effect on fertility, working animals, and so on, are fixed capital. Other features, such as physical immobility, may often characterize fixed capital, but not always. A ship is fixed capital, but is not immobile. Only productive capital is divided into fixed and circulating capital, since only productive capital can transfer or produce any value at all. A completed machine awaiting sale is commodity-capital, and cannot be included in either fixed or circulating capital until it is put to use.

The turnover time of fixed capital lasts for several turnovers of circulating capital. A portion of its value enters the product in each cycle of circulating capital, but the fixed capital is only replaced materially when it reaches the end of its life.

Section 2. Components, replacement, repair and accumulation of fixed capital

Repair and replacement introduce some complications in calculating the turnover period of fixed capital, which Marx deals with by making some (rather arbitrary) distinctions. In the simplest case, a complete item of fixed capital is replaced after a certain time, which differs between different pieces of fixed capital. The life of a piece of equipment is determined by wear and tear in use, deterioration from the mere passage of time, and 'moral depreciation' resulting from the competition of newer and better types of equipment. In some cases, components are periodically replaced, and this may be combined with (but must be distinguished from) piecemeal extensions. Piecemeal replacements and extensions may be financed out of the money reserve-fund accumulated to provide for replacement.

Maintenance, by contrast, is a necessary expense in each cycle of production and should be treated as an advance of circulating capital, like other current costs. Marx counts insurance against disasters as a deduction from surplus-value; how disasters and repairs are distinguished is unclear, but it probably makes little difference, since the capitalist pays anyway.

The capitalist must accumulate a hoard of money during the life of a piece of fixed capital, to provide for its eventual replacement. This 'sinking-fund' is built up steadily, then thrown back into circulation all at once when the replacement is paid for. A part of the money in existence is constantly being accumulated and laid out again by individual capitalists. On a wider scale, it is constantly being redistributed between the sinking-funds of different capitalists. In a credit system, to be discussed later, such temporarily idle funds can be mobilized to serve as active capital.

Chapter 9. The aggregate turnover of advanced capital. Cycles of turnover

Fixed and circulating capital have different turnover periods. The aggregate turnover of any capital is the average turnover time of its constituent parts. The average number of turnovers per year is calculated by taking the capital turned over in one year and dividing it by the advanced capital.

An example (mine, not Marx's) may make the principle clearer. Suppose a capitalist advances £10,000 to buy fixed capital equipment, with a life of ten years, and £1,000 in circulating capital which is turned over twenty-one times in a year. The capital advanced, then, is £11,000. The capital turned over in one year is one tenth of the fixed capital (£1,000) plus twenty-one times the circulating capital (£21,000), amounting to £22,000. The average number of turnovers is £22,000 ÷ £11,000, or 2. It is as if the capital of £11,000 had all been turned over twice in the year, with a turnover time of six months.

Chapter 10. Theories of fixed and circulating capital. The physiocrats and Adam Smith

In Marx's framework only production and, in production, only variable capital, produces surplus-value. The distinction between constant capital and variable capital is essential. The distinction between fixed and circulating capital plays a quite different role, related to turnover time. Marx turns aside now to criticize his predecessors for getting these distinctions wrong.

Quesnay, the physiocrat (often praised by Marx), only considered agricultural capital, since the physiocrats considered agriculture to be the only productive sector of the economy, but otherwise got the distinction between fixed and circulating capital about right.

Smith made a major advance, by extending the idea to all industries, but otherwise spread a great deal of confusion (according to Marx). Smith confused circulating capital in production with capital in circulation (money-capital, commodity-capital), and the production of surplus-value with its realization by sale of the product. He also gave the impression that the property of being fixed or circulating capital is inherent in particular things, rather than being a result of the role they play in the production process. Marx is frequently critical of Smith's treatment of the role of means of production.

Chapter 11. Theories of fixed and circulating capital. Ricardo

Ricardo identified fixed capital with instruments of production, and circulating capital with wage payments. He thus confused fixed capital with constant capital, circulating capital with variable capital, and made the critical distinction between means of production and labour-power a mere matter of turnover time. Marx is particularly disappointed, since Ricardo seemed to be on the right track with his labour theory of value.

The confusion of variable with circulating capital led Ricardo to think of all capital advances as purchases of material goods; fixed capital consists of means of production and circulating capital of means of subsistence (for the workers). This leads to a fetishized conception in which profit is generated by stocks of material goods, whereas Marx insists that it is the social relation between capitalist and worker that is the source of profit.

Chapter 12. The working period

Compare two branches of production, one (say cotton spinning) which produces a completed output each day or week, and another (say a locomotive works) that only produces a finished product after a whole series of activities lasting a longer time, a *working period*, such as a hundred days. Even if both involve the same daily expenditure on circulating capital (wages, materials), the first will recoup its advances quickly, while a larger capital will be required in the second case to continue paying wages and other costs over the longer period involved. The length of the working period only determines the circulating capital required, since fixed capital lasts for several working periods anyway.

Marx's terminology is slightly confusing. He talks of the two branches 'employing' the same capital, meaning the same flow (daily, weekly) of capital advances. He also speaks of 'capitals of equal size . . . invested' in the two branches, but says that the 'magnitude of the outlay of capital' is different. It is sometimes difficult to tell when he is talking of the *flow* of advances and when he means the *total* capital required.

Given the scale of the activity (the daily flow of spending), the capital required is directly proportional to the length of the working period. Projects with a long gestation period used to be beyond the scope of the individual capitalist and were carried out either by the state or by an individual capitalist serving as a mere contractor and receiving periodic progress payments. The concentration of capital into larger units makes these arrangements less necessary. The progress of capitalism also tends to shorten the working period by speeding up production, but at the same time fixed capital becomes more important, which tends to lengthen the average turnover period.

Chapter 13. The time of production

The *time of production* (from the start of work to the completion of a saleable product) may exceed the time during which actual work is being done, if some technically necessary pause intervenes. For example, pottery must dry, crops take time to grow, and so on. Intervals of this sort lengthen the turnover time of capital.

Chapter 14. The time of circulation

It takes time to sell products and to transform the resulting money capital into productive capital again. The *time of circulation* must be included in the turnover time of capital. Different branches of production and different capitals within the same branch will be subject to varying delays.

Transport time, the time required to ship goods to customers and to remit the proceeds back, is one major factor, but is reduced by improvements in transport. When goods are delivered in bulk, a shipment must be accumulated over a period of time, which is equivalent to a lengthening of the time of production.

There are also delays in the reconversion of money-capital into productive capital. When supplies are only available at intervals, or are uncertain, reserves of money and stocks of goods must be held, tying up capital unproductively and lengthening the turnover.

Chapter 15. Effect of the time of turnover on the magnitude of advanced capital

The circuit of capital consists of a period of production followed by a period of circulation. Normally, production continues uninterrupted, so additional capital has to be advanced at the end of a period of production in order to continue producing while awaiting the proceeds of the sale of the preceding period's output.

In investigating this issue, Marx gets enmeshed in a series of rather unnecessary numerical examples. Engels, as editor, comments on these and reports that what he published is only an abridged version of a worse mess that Marx left him. There is some interest in seeing Marx at work, grimly determined to leave no stone unturned, though the reader's patience may not last to the end of the chapter. It is hard to believe that Marx would have published the material in this form had he lived to complete the work.

The main points are established with an example in which £100 is advanced per week in production, with a turnover time of nine weeks, divided in various ways between the time of production and the time of circulation. Fixed capital is ignored, and so is surplus-value. We might think of the example as a case of simple reproduction in which surplus-value is skimmed off to be spent on consumer goods, outside the scope of the discussion of turnover.

The main results are much less complicated than they seem. Firstly, if production is to continue for nine weeks at a weekly cost of £100, then a capital outlay of £900 will be required. At the end of nine weeks the first proceeds return and can be ploughed back.

Secondly, with a 'year' of fifty-one weeks, there are $5\frac{2}{3}$ turnovers per year ($51 \div 9$). Marx gets various slightly different answers because he considers the first year, so parts of the capital do not start functioning until after the start of the year. If he had considered a year in the life of an already functioning capital, he would have arrived at $5\frac{2}{3}$ turnovers per year in all cases.

Thirdly, the proceeds will return at the end of each turnover as a lump sum, but will be spent bit by bit (in the example, £100 each week). Therefore, a considerable part of the total capital will be tied up as money-capital for much of the time. Marx will return to this point in discussing credit, since idle sums of money can be mobilized through the banking system.

Section 1. The working period equal to the circulation period

In this case, capital is laid out for four and a half weeks at the weekly rate of £100. When the first production period is complete, a second starts; when the second ends, the proceeds of the first become available to start production again. It is as if two independent capitals alternated places in production and circulation.

Section 2. The working period greater than the period of circulation

Let the working period be six weeks, and the circulation period three weeks. At the end of each working period, additional capital is laid out for three weeks to keep production going until the proceeds of the previous period come in.

Section 3. The working period smaller than the circulation period

If the working period is short relative to the circulation period, several batches of the product will have to be completed and put into the circulation pipeline before the proceeds of the first return. Once the proceeds start coming in, they do so more frequently and in smaller amounts than would be the case with a longer working period.

Section 4. Conclusions

A reduction in the time of circulation, and hence in turnover time, will release capital (reduce capital required), while an increase (for example, in a crisis when goods become hard to sell) ties up extra capital.

Section 5. The effect of a change in prices

A fall in the prices of the means of production and labour-power will reduce weekly outlay and capital required. An increase would have the opposite effect. There are gains (losses) for the capitalist if the price of the product rises (falls).

Chapter 16. The turnover of variable capital

Section 1. The annual rate of surplus-value

The *annual rate of surplus-value* is the surplus-value generated in a year, divided by the size of the variable capital advanced. The surplus-value generated in each turnover is determined by the rate of surplus-value (without the qualifier 'annual') as defined in volume one. To get the annual rate, Marx multiplies the rate of surplus-value by the number of turnovers per year.

Section 2. The turnover of the individual variable capital

With the help of an example, Marx spells out how wages are advanced, spent by workers, and reconstituted as capital at the end of the turnover period, through the sale of the workers' product.

Section 3. The turnover of the variable capital from the social point of view

Where turnover is rapid, relatively little capital is required because costs are soon covered by the sale of the product.

A 'communistic' society would have to make decisions about how much resources to allocate to projects with a long gestation period. These activities subtract 'labour, means of production and means of subsistence from the total annual production' (p. 35) without providing a return to society for a considerable period. Society must calculate in advance how large a fraction of its resources it can afford to tie up in this way. In this section, Marx recognizes that there is a real social cost to the use of more 'capital intensive' (in the non-Marxist sense) methods of production. Critics have not often realized this; admittedly Marx's comments are hidden in a fairly inconspicuous part of *Capital*.

In a capitalist society no co-ordinated calculation is carried out, and 'great disturbances may and must constantly occur' (p. 315). An easy money market encourages enterprises with long gestation periods, which put pressure on the market by requiring large advances of money once started.

Once large scale investments are under way, they generate large demands for materials, for labour-power, and for means of subsistence (bought by the newly employed workers), pushing up prices and wages and creating the conditions for a collapse. A non-Marxist economist might respond by saying that as money gets scarce and wages rise, investment will be discouraged, and an equilibrium established. Marx's point is presumably that once a project with a long gestation period is started, an interruption is very disruptive.

A footnote records a note inserted in the manuscript for future amplification. 'Contradiction in the capitalist mode of production: the labourers as buyers of commodities are important for the market. But as sellers of their own commodity – labour-power – capitalist society tends to keep them down to the minimum price . . . [T]he sale of commodities . . . is limited . . . by the consumer requirements of a society in which the vast majority are always poor' (p. 316n). This can be set alongside similar passing comments, and contrasted with other comments to the effect that it is high, not low, wages that precede a crisis. In the text, Marx has just explained how rising wages and prices can lead to a crisis. Marx did not present a connected account of crises anywhere in *Capital*.

In a final remark, Marx points out that market conditions affect the length of the turnover. When prices are falling (in a crisis, for example) supplies are deliberately held back in the hope of a recovery, thus lengthening the time of circulation.

Chapter 17. The circulation of surplus-value

Despite its title, the final chapter of part two is mainly concerned with the circulation of money. It is made up of a number of fragments, and contains digressions, such as quotations from Thompson asserting that the real wealth of a country consists of its annual production, and that accumulated wealth is significant mainly in giving the owners of wealth a claim over the annual produce. In Marx's terms, this means that ownership of wealth is what allows capitalists to capture part of the product of other people's work.

Section 1. Simple reproduction

Simple reproduction is an analytical fiction that Marx uses repeatedly. Production is assumed to remain constant and capitalists spend all of surplus-value on individual consumption, while keeping their accumulated capital intact.

In this context, assuming that all circulating money consists of actual gold and silver, Marx tackles two questions. Firstly, what is the function of the producers of precious metals? Secondly, are there any special problems in analysing the circulation of money in a capitalist system, as distinct from a simple commodity producing system? These are really two separate questions, but they tend to get mixed up together in Marx's presentation.

Marx treats gold production as the direct production of money, so that the circuit of capital in gold production is $M - C \ldots P \ldots M'$. Otherwise, the gold producer is just like any other capitalist, producing commodities and surplus-value. Gold is, of course, assumed to exchange at its value.

In simple reproduction, the mass of commodities produced and exchanged remains constant from year to year, so the amount of money required in circulation remains constant. Newly produced gold is needed only to replace wear and tear of existing coins, and to provide for non-monetary uses, such as the production of jewellery. Enough gold will be produced to meet this demand, just as enough is produced of any commodity to meet the needs of reproduction.

Marx then takes up a question raised by an unnamed 'opponent of Tooke'. If the capitalist pays out a certain amount of money $(c + v)$, how can he get back more $(c + v + s)$? Where does the money come from? After dismissing various attempts to answer the question by tricks of one sort or another, Marx shows that no problem exists. In simple reproduction, the capitalists, as a class, advance $c + v$ as capital and spend s on individual consumption, and they then sell the product of the new cycle of production for $c + v + s$, regaining from circulation exactly what they had put into circulation. In the following period they spend the same and get it back, and so on. Money circulates just as in simple commodity circulation. All of this will be dealt with in more detail in part three.

Another problem is now posed, which has little to do with what has gone before. What happens if wages rise? Workers' demand for necessities, and the more modest luxuries, will increase, but at the same time capitalists' demand for the grosser luxuries will fall. Resources will be transferred from industries that supply capitalists to those that meet workers' needs.

Marx's aim here is to counteract the idea that wage increases are futile because they would only cause price increases, with no gain to the workers. He argues that prices in general should not rise, since capitalists' demand will fall by as much as workers' demand increases. If capitalists could raise prices they would do so, whether wages rose or not.

He adds some further comments on wages and prices. An increase in the price of necessities may cause a wage increase (rather than vice-versa). A wage increase in a particular industry on its own may raise the price of the products of that industry. A general wage increase would cause an increase in prices in industries employing a high proportion of variable to constant capital, but would reduce prices in other industries. The latter two cases rest on theory that will not be explained until volume three, part two. The point here is that these cases may mislead observers into thinking that a general wage increase would cause a general price increase.

To finish the section there is a brief discussion of the relation between the velocity of circulation of money and the turnover of capital. The two are, of course, quite distinct. It is true that a more rapid turnover of capital tends to speed the circulation of money, but the velocity of circulation of money may equally be increased by other factors, such as improvements in the technical arrangements for transferring money, that have nothing to do with the turnover of capital.

Section 2. Accumulation and reproduction on an extended scale

Accumulation, the normal state of affairs in a functioning capitalist economy, takes place when part or all of surplus-value is advanced as new capital instead of being spent on individual consumption. The main lines of analysis are the same as for simple reproduction. Since the mass of commodities produced and sold is increasing as time passes, additional money will be needed in circulation, unless ways can be found to economize on the money required (by increasing the velocity of circulation) or unless enough money is released from hoards. The extra money comes from gold production. (In a modern paper-money system, of course, the money would simply be printed.) Production of gold absorbs real resources (labour-power, means of production), and must be counted as one of the social costs (*faux frais*) of the capitalist system of production. Hoards of money are accumulated, ready for investment in productive capital, and then released. If capitalists accumulate claims on others (bank deposits, securities) instead of idle money balances, the money is passed on to others who use it.

PART 3

The reproduction and circulation of the aggregate social capital

Chapter 18. Introduction

Section 1. The subject investigated

The reproduction of capital is a circular process, continually renewed, in which commodities embodying surplus-value are produced and sold, and then means of production and labour-power are bought to renew the process again. So far, Marx has analysed production and reproduction mainly from the viewpoint of an individual capitalist who is assumed to succeed in selling his product and to find the required means of production and labour-power available in the market.

Each individual capital, however, is only a fraction of the total social capital. In the final part of volume two, which is in many ways the culmination of his economic analysis, Marx investigates the reproduction of the total social capital. From this viewpoint it is not enough to look at the reproduction of capital in value terms; the material elements of capital must also be reproduced. The production of different commodities must match the demand for them. If means of production are to be purchased, they must have been produced. If labour-power is to be available, workers must be able to spend their wages on the consumer goods that they need. The total process of social production must mesh with the total process of commodity exchange. The main issues are dealt with in the context of simple reproduction in chapter twenty, which is the centrepiece of the analysis. Some preliminaries are disposed of first.

Section 2. The role of money-capital

The discussion of money-capital is a digression, and contributes little to the argument. Money-capital is the starting point of every individual capital, and the funds available limit the scale on which production can take place. The scale of individual units of production can grow, whatever the growth of the total social capital, through the centralization of capital and through the development of the credit system.

Chapter 19. Former presentations of the subject

Marx starts by criticizing his predecessors. The main charge against them here is of simple confusion, rather than ideological bias, so the discussion is of rather limited interest to modern readers unfamiliar with the work of Quesnay, Smith, and so on. In the course of his critique, Marx recapitulates substantial parts of his own theory.

Section 1. The physiocrats

Quesnay's *Tableau Economique* was a major source of inspiration for Marx. It set out, in broad outline, the way in which the annual product of agriculture could be divided between different uses, and redistributed by exchange, so as to reproduce the process of prod-duction. Marx, of course, aims to do the same for the whole social product, not just for agriculture. In particular, Quesnay was aware that a part of the product had to be retained for use in production (as seed corn, for example), a point which escaped Adam Smith. Smith counted seed corn as fixed capital, on the grounds that it was not sold, and therefore did not 'circulate'. As has been seen, Smith con-fused circulating capital with the process of circulation (exchange).

Section 2. Adam Smith

According to Marx, Smith came close to a correct analysis at some points, but lapsed into confusion. Firstly, Smith confused the production of use-values with the production of exchange-value, for example by arguing that nature produces exchange-value (in agriculture).

Secondly, Smith argued that the value of the product is determined by the wages, profits and rents derived from it, confusing the source of value with the distribution of income between different kinds of incomes. It is as if he claimed that a cake was large because it was cut into certain slices, instead of recognizing that it is the size of the cake that limits the size of the slices.

Thirdly, Smith argues that the whole value of the product can be divided into wages, profits and rents, $v + s$ in Marx's terms, ignoring the part of the value of the product that replaces the value of means of production used up, c. Smith defends this argument in several ways. First, he distinguishes net ('neat') from gross revenue, but falls into inconsistencies. He also argues that the value of the means of production used up can itself be resolved into wages, profits and rents paid out in previous periods. This causes difficulties because it is necessary to distinguish revenues currently paid out (and available to be spent on buying this year's product) from revenues paid out in previous periods.

Whether Smith was really this confused is open to doubt. Marx was not a generous critic of the works of other writers.

Section 3. Later economists

Smith's successors failed to sort out all of these confusions. Ricardo regarded wages and profits as a division of the value of the product and not as sources of value (correctly, according to Marx), but still treated the value of the output as wholly resolvable into wages and profits, just as Smith did.

Chapter 20. Simple reproduction

The chapter on simple reproduction is the centrepiece of Marx's analysis of reproduction. It is somewhat repetitive, with some breaks in the continuity of the argument, partly because it was assembled by Engels from two separate manuscripts.

Section 1. The formulation of the question

The annual product consists of various parts, some of which replace capital (i.e. replace the means of production) while others go to the consumption-fund to be consumed by (and thus reproduce) the capitalist and working classes. To analyse the reproduction of the social capital it is necessary to show how its component parts are reproduced, both in value and in material terms. It will be assumed that commodities exchange at their values, and that reproduction takes place on a constant scale with all surplus-value spent on individual consumption.

Section 2. The two departments of social production

Marx divides output into two categories, and correspondingly divides the economy into two 'departments': department I, which produces means of production, and department II, which produces articles of consumption.

As Marx has shown in volume one, the value of the output of each department can be divided into three parts. One part, c, corresponds to the value of the means of production used up. The new value added in the cycle of production that has just ended, $v + s$, is made up of the value of the labour-power employed, v, and the surplus-value that accrues to the capitalist, s. It will help to understand the argument if we think of the output of each department being divided into three heaps of products, with values equal to c, v and s respectively (as in volume one, chapter nine, section two).

Reproduction of the value of capital requires that a buyer be found for each of the six parts of the social product (three in each department). For the material elements of production to be reproduced, each department must acquire means of production corresponding to those used up, and must purchase labour-power on the same scale as in the preceding year. An annual cycle of production is implicitly assumed. Fixed capital, which is only replaced at intervals, is ignored for the moment; it will be discussed in section eleven.

Marx next sets out a numerical example, which will be used throughout the chapter. The examples used in this chapter and the next are often referred to as 'schemes' or 'schemas' of reproduction.

The output of department I, that is, the newly produced output of means of production, has a value of 6,000, made up of 4,000 c + 1,000 v + 1,000 s, where 4,000 c stands for a constant capital of 4,000, and so on. The numbers stand for pounds, dollars, or whatever; the example is hypothetical. The product of department II is 2,000 c + 500 v + 500 s = 3,000.

In tabular form, for easy reference, the example is:

I.   4,000 c + 1,000 v + 1,000 s = 6,000,

II. 2,000 c +   500 v +   500 s = 3,000.

In a few paragraphs, Marx sets out all the salient points of his analysis. They will be repeated many times in more detail and from different angles, in subsequent sections.

The constant capital used up in the two departments (4,000 + 2,000) must be replaced, so there is a demand for means of production with a value of 6,000, exactly matching the supply of means of production, the output of department I. By assumption, all of variable capital (wages) and surplus-value is spent on articles of consumption, making a demand of 3,000 (1,000 + 1,000 + 500 + 500), again exactly matching supply.

Consider each department as an integrated whole (i.e. ignoring transactions inside each department), in order to focus on exchanges between departments. Department I uses 4,000 of its own product (to replace c) leaving a surplus of 2,000 to be sold to department II. At the same time, 1,000 of department II's product is consumed by workers and capitalists within department II, leaving a surplus of 2,000 to be sold to department I. So department I sells goods with a value of 2,000 to department II and buys goods of exactly the same value in exchange. Reproduction can proceed smoothly.

Each participant in exchange receives money and spends exactly the amount received. Workers get wages and spend them. Capitalists spend (as capital advances or for individual consumption) exactly what they get by the sale of the product. Each therefore ends up with the same amount of money as at the beginning, ready to repeat the process indefinitely.

Section 3. Exchange between the two departments

Means of production worth 2,000 are sold by department I to department II, in exchange for an equal value in articles of consumption. Marx makes some arbitrary assumptions about the order of transactions in order to trace the circulation of money. Many similar stories could be told.

The capitalists in department I pay wages of £1,000 (the pound sign, £, signals a money payment) to the workers in that department, who buy consumer goods, passing the £1,000 on to the capitalists of department II. The latter can now buy means of production with a value of £1,000, returning the money to its starting point in department I. Half the exchange is completed.

Means of production with a value of 1,000 remain to be exchanged for 1,000 in consumer goods. Marx assumes that the capitalists in II have £500 which they spend on means of production, and the capitalists in I return the money by buying consumer goods. Simultaneously, the capitalists in I have £500 available, which they spend on consumer goods, enabling the department II capitalists to complete the replacement of their means of production by buying the rest of department I's saleable output. The exchange is complete, and all the money is back where it started. The details are arbitrary; provided someone has enough money, the exchange can go through. Money to the value of £2,000 (count it) has allowed the exchange of goods worth a total of £4,000 plus labour-power to the value of £1,000.

For uninterrupted reproduction then, $v + s$ in department I must match c in department II; spending on consumer goods by workers and capitalists in department I must equal spending on means of production by department II. We should still ask, why should the two be equal? Marx passes over the question very briefly.

The key requirement for reproduction is that the total social capital should be correctly divided between the two departments. The ratios between c, v and s in each department can be taken as given for analytical purposes; s/v is determined by the value of labour-power and the working-day, c/v by the technology of production and the values of commodities. With these ratios fixed, an increase (or decrease) in the scale of department I will increase (or decrease) $v + s$ in that department, and similarly any change in department II will alter c in department II. If $v + s$ in I exceeded c in II, then capital would have to be transferred from I to II in order to reach the necessary balance, and so on. Such a transfer would not, of course, normally take place smoothly but would involve a crisis, a temporary breakdown in reproduction.

What Marx demonstrates is that it is logically possible for a capitalist society to reproduce itself, not that it will always do so smoothly.

Section 4. Exchange within department II

Department II produces a variety of goods. Marx divides it into two parts: IIa, which produces necessities, and IIb, which produces luxuries consumed by capitalists but not by workers. Subsequent Marxist writers have often relabelled IIa and IIb as departments two and three, respectively. The division between IIa and IIb is only an example of the further subdivisions between different branches within department II that could be considered.

Workers in IIa produce the goods they themselves consume; they are paid wages, spend them on their own products, and the money flows straight back to their employers. Workers in department IIb, like those in department I, do not produce the goods they consume. They spend their wages on products of IIa, and the money flows back to the capitalists of IIb when IIa capitalists buy luxury products of IIb. Given appropriate relative scales of production in the two parts of department II, reproduction can proceed. Marx works through a numerical example, which is repeated in the following section.

The section concludes with a short but important digression on crises. In a crisis the demand for luxuries shrinks both absolutely and relatively while demand increases in periods of prosperity when the working class 'enjoys momentarily articles of luxury ordinarily beyond its reach' (p. 410).

Crises are caused by, or rather, consist of, a depression of demand, a 'scarcity of effective consumers'. This is a tautology, a description of a crisis and not an explanation of why crises occur. If one argues that crises are caused by the poverty of the workers, and hence their inability to purchase their own products, one must reckon with the fact that 'crises are always prepared by precisely a period in which wages rise generally and the working class actually gets a larger share of that part of the annual product which is intended for consumption' (p. 411). Demand comes from capitalists as well as workers, as the schemes of reproduction show. The capitalist gets a profit because the workers get less than the value that they produce; the goods that workers produce and cannot afford to buy are bought by their employers. Exploitation is not a cause of crisis, but a necessity for capitalist reproduction. Many subsequent Marxists have adopted the 'underconsumptionist' theory that Marx warns against, and have tried to explain crises in terms of the workers' lack of purchasing power.

Section 5. The mediation of exchange by the circulation of money

Marx works through the circulation of money, again, twice, to stress the point that money only serves as a vehicle for the exchange of commodities, and that all the money involved returns to its starting point ready for the next cycle. The subordinate (though necessary) role of money in the circulation of capital is obscured, in practice, by the intervention of merchant's capital and independent money-capital (financial capital), and also by the division of surplus-value into various kinds of income (rent, interest, etc.).

Section 6. The constant capital of Department I

Part of the means of production produced in department I must be kept in the department to replace constant capital used up. Individual enterprises, however, do not usually produce the means of production that they themselves use, so exchange takes place between different enterprises in department I.

Section 7. Variable capital and surplus-value in both departments

Marx now returns to his criticism of Adam Smith, and spends several sections clarifying the difference between Smith's analysis and his own. In simple reproduction, the total new value produced, the sum of $v + s$ in both departments, is equal to the whole (gross) output of department II, the output of consumer goods. This must be so, since all of v and s are spent on consumer goods. For this reason, Smith was able to maintain the idea that all of net output consists of consumer goods, and that all of the value of (net) output can be resolved into v and s. Not all the new value added, however, is added in department II (only ⅓ is, in Marx's example). Since the means of production used up are exactly replaced (simple reproduction), net output consists only of consumer goods.

Section 8. The constant capital in both departments

Smith's confusion over net and gross output arises from a failure to distinguish the value of the product from its material character. Both departments reproduce the *value* of the means of production that they consume, and both add new value to their product. In terms of the *material* basis of reproduction, department I reproduces the means of production used up in both departments, while department II does not reproduce the material elements of the means of production that it uses, but produces all of society's consumer goods. Hence the exchange between them.

Section 9. A retrospect to Adam Smith, Storch and Ramsey

Smith argued that the entire value of the product could be resolved into wages, profits and rents, $v + s$, since the value of the means of production used up can be resolved into value added ($v + s$) in earlier stages of production. So long as we only look at the final goods that correspond to net output, i.e. to goods that are not used to replace used up means of production, their value will be equal to $v + s$ for the whole system (because the goods that are used to replace c have a value equal to c). If we were to count the values of all goods, they would exceed $v + s$. Although Marx does not say so, Smith's net product approach could be made completely consistent, both with itself and with Marx's analysis, and is the basis of modern national income accounts. Marx's complaint against Smith is that he is neither clear nor consistent.

Section 10. Capital and revenue: variable capital and wages

Marx now turns to confusions caused by misuse of the terms 'capital' and 'revenue'. Roughly speaking, 'capital' is a fund that must be maintained intact, while 'revenue' is a flow of income that may be spent on consumption. Speaking roughly, however, is liable to lead to mistakes.

From a social point of view, in terms of use-values, means of production must be replaced, and the rest of output can be consumed. From the point of view of the individual capitalist, in terms of exchange-values, the value of advanced capital must be reproduced, while surplus-value is a revenue that can be consumed.

There are two sources of confusion here. Firstly, means of production are produced for sale, and the capitalist who sells them gets revenue (surplus-value) in the process, although from the point of view of use-values his whole product is used to replace (another capitalist's) constant capital. Secondly, wage payments are advances of capital, but are revenue to the workers. The point is that each individual capital goes through the metamorphoses set out in part one of this volume. Money is advanced as capital to buy means of production and labour-power. When the exchange is completed, the original capital remains intact in the hands of its original owner, in the form of productive capital. The money is simply the vehicle of the exchange, and now serves as revenue to the worker, who had no capital before, and still has none. The worker's purchase of consumer goods is a spending of revenue.

Section 11. Replacement of the fixed capital

The analysis so far has been based on the assumption that the constant capital used up is replaced during the year. Fixed capital, however, is replaced at intervals, and in the meantime a money reserve is built up to pay for replacement. Marx makes very heavy weather of the problem of incorporating fixed capital into his account of reproduction.

Some pieces of fixed capital are not replaced during a given year, so their owners add an amount equivalent to the value lost during the year to their reserve-funds. Other items are replaced, so their owners spend the depreciation-funds accumulated in previous periods. The former sell more than they buy, the latter buy more than they sell. If the two exactly offset each other there is no problem.

If, however, a larger than normal amount of fixed capital is replaced in a particular year, replacement purchases will exceed depreciation allowances, and department I would have to be larger than the analysis so far would suggest, in order to provide the replacement equipment. If a smaller than normal part of fixed capital is replaced in the year, a smaller department I would be needed. Clearly, uneven replacement of fixed capital from year to year is incompatible with smooth simple reproduction.

Under normal conditions hoards of money exist in depreciation funds. The money is repeatedly released from one fund, when equipment is replaced, and this is offset by the withdrawal of money from circulation, into other replacement funds.

Section 12. Reproduction of the money material

In Marx's analysis, money is gold, and he assumes that it is produced within the economy concerned (if it is imported, goods of equal value must be produced and exported in exchange). Gold production is counted in department I, 'like that of metals generally' (p. 470). Some later Marxists include it in department IIb, or three. The discussion of chapter seventeen, showing that gold production has no special significance, is rehearsed again.

In the analysis of this section (as in chapter seventeen), it seems that gold is produced in excess of that needed to offset current wear and tear on coins, so that money is being added to hoards. Strictly, this is incompatible with simple reproduction in which everything continues unchanged from one year to the next, but it makes little difference since the addition of gold to hoards is economically equivalent to the purchase of luxury goods.

Section 13. Destutt de Tracy's theory of reproduction

Destutt de Tracy thought, according to Marx, that capitalists made profits by selling goods above their value. Marx rejects the theory.

Chapter 21. Accumulation and reproduction on an extended scale

Simple reproduction is an analytical fiction; in real capitalist societies accumulation is the norm. The chapter on accumulation clearly gave Marx a considerable amount of difficulty, and remains unfinished.

When an individual capitalist accumulates, he first builds up a hoard of money, then advances it as capital to buy extra constant capital (and, Marx should have added, variable capital). On a social level the building-up of hoards is not accumulation at all, though a general build-up of hoards would be possible if gold production exceeded wear and tear of coins.

Additional means of production can only be bought if they have already been produced. The material concomitant of accumulation is an enlargement of department I to provide the necessary means of production.

Section 1. Accumulation in department I

Marx is sidetracked by the building-up of hoards of money; the issue is the same as that involved in the replacement of fixed capital, which has already been dealt with. Some capitalists (A, A', etc.) are building up hoards, while others (B, B' etc.) are spending their hoarded money on productive capital. The two must balance each other, or reproduction will be disrupted. Sufficient money must exist for the active circulation and for reserve hoards. It is assumed that additional labour-power is freely available.

Section 2. Accumulation in department II

If the proportions between the two departments remain the same as in simple reproduction, while capitalists try to buy more means of production (to expand production) and less consumer goods, the result will be a surplus of unsaleable consumer goods. Marx finds this out the hard way, by working through an example.

Section 3. Schematic presentation of accumulation

Marx makes a few false starts. His first example, labelled schemes (a) and (b), does not work, so he tries again, setting out the scheme for simple reproduction (A) and a revised scheme for accumulation (B). In setting up scheme B, he arbitrarily changes the ratio of c to v from that in scheme A; in reality, for an economy to expand, department I would have to be expanded relative to the size that would be right for simple reproduction. In hypothetical examples one can, of course, change anything.

Scheme B can now be set in motion. Marx assumes that half of surplus-value in department I is accumulated, with the ratio c/v held constant. His example (scheme B) is:

$$\text{I. } 4,000\,c + 1,000\,v + 1,000\,s = 6,000,$$
$$\text{II. } 1,500\,c + 750\,v + 750\,s = 3,000.$$

Half of the $1,000\,s$ is accumulated in I, so an additional capital of 500 ($400\,c + 100\,v$) is advanced in department I, which now uses 4,400 of its own product (4,000 replacement of c + 400 additional c), leaving 1,600 to be sold to department II. (Marx's presentation is confusing; he writes out the uses of the product as if they were components of value.)

In order to get the story going, Marx assumes that department II always passively buys whatever means of production department I makes available: a rather strange assumption. Accumulation in department II is governed by the available means of production, and capitalists spend the part of surplus-value that is not accumulated on individual consumption. There is nothing in the working of a capitalist system to induce this sort of co-operative behaviour; if anything the assumption might be more appropriate for a planned economy. Given this assumption, it is not surprising that accumulation proceeds smoothly.

Department II buys 1,600 in means of production from department I, of which 1,500 represents replacement of c, so that an additional c of 100 is advanced in department II, and an additional v of 50 (to keep c/v constant). Demand for means of production balances supply, by assumption, so the demand and supply of consumer goods must balance too. Checking the demand and supply of consumer goods: workers spend what they get, which is 1,100 (the new v in I) plus 800 (the new v in II), and capitalists spend what they do not accumulate, 500 (in I) plus 600 (in II). Total demand for consumer goods is 3,000, which exactly matches the output of department II.

Having worked out how accumulation proceeds in the first period, Marx can write down how things stand in the next:

I. $4,400\,c + 1,100\,v + 1,100\,s = 6,600$,

II. $1,600\,c + \quad 800\,v + \quad 800\,s = 3,200$.

where s/v is assumed to stay the same. He now works through another cycle, and so on, until he has worked through five successive years. After a while, the two departments grow in line with each other, a result that flows directly from the extraordinary assumptions made. If department II always absorbs any surplus of means of production, it will grow rapidly when department I is large, because a large department I will provide a large surplus, and department II will grow slowly when department I is relatively small. The relative scale of the two departments adjusts automatically. It should be emphasized again that this is a wholly artificial case.

Marx works through a second example on similar lines, adds a few general comments, and proceeds no further.

He has shown that expanded reproduction is logically possible, and his method can be used to examine various possible assumptions to find out whether they are consistent with continued accumulation or not. Numerical examples, however, are not an adequate method, since one never knows whether the results are generally true or whether they are the outcome of a lucky choice of numbers to start with.

Section 4. Supplementary remarks

Accumulation requires enough money to allow the formation of hoards awaiting capitalization. The money comes from gold producers, who exchange their product for the products of other industries. Marx has already discussed hoards in department I, and he now shows that hoards in department II perform much the same function. It is a limp ending to the volume, which was, of course, left unfinished by Marx.

The process of capitalist production as a whole

The conversion of surplus-value into profit and of the rate of surplus-value into the rate of profit

The analysis of capitalism presented in the first two volumes of *Capital* is based on the simplifying assumption that prices are proportional to values, so that commodities are exchanged for an equal value in money. Each capital is a representative fraction of capital as a whole, and the surplus-value accruing to each capitalist is the result of the surplus-labour performed by the workers that he himself employs.

Volume three deals with the way in which surplus-value is divided up into the categories of property income that are encountered in everyday life: profits, interest and rent. Marx's argument is that these are all forms of surplus-value, and are therefore ultimately explained by the analysis of surplus-value presented in volume one.

In the first part of volume three, prices are still assumed to be proportional to values, and Marx discusses how surplus-value appears to the capitalist. Costs of production, to the capitalist, are less than the selling price; the difference is *profit*. The capitalist is not concerned with the rate of surplus-value, but with the *rate of profit*, profit divided by capital advanced. This part lays the groundwork for the analysis of the equalization of profit rates (part two) and of the tendency of the rate of profit to fall (part three).

Throughout volume three, Marx returns to the theme of 'appearances'. Profit 'appears' to be produced by the whole of capital advanced, rent by land, and so on. These statements should always be interpreted as saying that things appear in a certain way, to a superficial observer ignorant of Marx's analysis, but really they

127

are quite different. Profit and rent, for example, are the result of the exploitation of the workers. Marx's comments on 'appearances' are, of course, a development of the idea of 'fetishism' introduced in the first chapter of volume one.

Chapter 1. Cost-price and profit

The actual cost of producing a commodity, according to Marx, is measured by the labour required, i.e. by the value of the commodity. The capitalist, however, counts only what he has to pay, the price of the necessary labour-power and means of production, $c + v$. Marx calls this the *cost-price* of the commodity. Where fixed capital is used, the cost-price includes wear and tear on the fixed capital.

The surplus-value received by the capitalist now appears as an addition to the cost-price, so that the selling price is $k + p$, where k is cost-price and p is profit. So long as prices are proportional to values, profit is simply another name for surplus-value. Marx uses the term to signify the gain to the capitalist whether it is equal to surplus-value or not. For example, goods could be sold below value and still yield a (reduced) profit. In part two, Marx will argue that goods are regularly sold at prices that differ from values, so that the profit of any individual capitalist differs from the surplus-value produced by 'his' workers. Profit appears either to be produced by all of the capital advanced, or by selling above cost (i.e. it appears this way to those who have not studied Marx's analysis); the special connection between surplus-value and labour is obliterated when profit is thought of in this way.

Chapter 2. The rate of profit

The capitalist advances money to make more money; that is the point of capitalist production. All that the capitalist cares about is the profit as a fraction of the total capital advanced. The *rate of profit* is the ratio of profit to capital advanced, p/C or, if goods exchange at their values, s/C, where C is the total capital advanced.

If capital turns over once a year, the annual rate of profit can be written as $s/(c + v)$. The source of profit is mystified in this form, since the whole of capital, not just variable capital, seems to be responsible for producing profit.

Chapter 3. The relation of the rate of profit to the rate of surplus-value

Writing $s' = s/v$ for the rate of surplus-value, and $p' = s/C$ for the rate of profit, we have $p' = s'v/C$, or $p' = s'v/(c + v)$. It is assumed that goods sell at their values, and that the turnover time is one year. Various factors that influence p' are taken as given: the value of money (changes in the value of money would cause paper gains or losses, and complicate matters), turnover time, the productivity and intensity of labour, the length of the working-day and the level of wages.

Marx next works through the effects of changes in s, v and c. The main result is that, given s', the rate of profit depends on v/C, which in turn depends on the value composition of capital c/v. The result is most easily seen by writing v/C as $v/(c + v)$ and dividing top and bottom of the fraction by v. Then $v/C = 1/(c/v + 1)$, so that $p' = s'/(c/v + 1)$.

The link between the rate of profit and the value composition of capital is of fundamental importance to the following two parts. In words, the rate of surplus-value measures the ratio of surplus-value to *variable* capital. The ratio of surplus-value to *total* capital depends on the rate of surplus-value and on the ratio of variable to total capital, and the latter ratio depends on the ratio of variable to constant capital. (It also depends on turnover time and hence on the ratio of fixed to circulating capital, a factor that Marx ignores at this stage.)

Chapter 4. The effect of turnover on the rate of profit

Marx left only the title of this chapter; the text was added by Engels. It is straightforward. The annual rate of surplus-value is the surplus-value produced per year divided by the variable capital advanced, and equals the rate of surplus-value multiplied by the number of turnovers of variable capital per year. (See volume two, chapter sixteen.)

Similarly, the rate of profit measures the annual profit as a fraction of the total capital required. If this definition is kept firmly in mind, the complications caused by varying turnover times present no difficulty. Marx's formula $p' = s'v/(c + v)$ can be very misleading, since the first v (in the numerator) represents the total outlay on variable capital during the year, while the v in the denominator represents the variable part of the total capital required; the two are only equal if the turnover time is one year. Engels gives the alternative formulation $p' = s'nv/C$, where n is the number of turnovers of variable capital and v the variable capital advanced in each turnover, so that $s'n\,v$ is the surplus-value generated per year, while C is the total capital required, including fixed capital.

Marx's treatment of turnover is very weak throughout volume three; the manuscript of this volume was actually written before the parts of volume two that deal with turnover time.

Chapter 5. Economy in the employment of constant capital

Economy in the use of constant capital will raise the rate of profit for a given rate of surplus-value, by reducing the total capital on which the profit is calculated. The main point of Marx's discussion of this issue is to lay some groundwork for analysing trends in the rate of profit.

Section 1. In general

The development of capitalism tends to lead to economies in the use of constant capital. A lengthening of the working-day increases the hours for which fixed capital is used. An expanding scale of production permits economies in buildings, power sources, and so on. Increasing productivity reduces the value of means of production.

The utilization of wastes as by-products is another saving. In the limit, if the constant capital used were reduced to zero, the (annual) rate of profit would be equal to the (annual) rate of surplus-value.

Since the capitalist wants to raise the rate of profit, while workers have no reason to care, economy must be enforced by harsh discipline, which 'will become superfluous under a social system in which the labourers work for their own account' (p. 83).

Despite all this, the mass of constant capital may grow both absolutely and relatively, since each worker will handle more equipment and materials as productivity increases. In deriving his 'law of the tendency of the rate of profit to fall' (part three, below), Marx assumes that c rises relative to v.

Section 2. Savings at the expense of the labourers

Costs may be reduced at the expense of the health and safety of the workers. Marx cites examples.

Section 3. Economy in the generation and transmission of power, and in buildings

A quotation from Naysmith (a famous engineer) serves as an example of the kind of economies referred to in the title of the section.

Section 4. Utilization of the excretions of production

Wastes of various sorts may be turned into valuable by-products. (This is not, strictly, an economy in the use of constant capital, but it fits conveniently into the discussion.)

Section 5. Economy through inventions

Large scale production and socialization of labour are the preconditions for the productive use of inventions that raise productivity and economize on constant capital. Marx distinguishes, in passing, between 'universal' and 'co-operative' labour. Universal labour is scientific research and discovery which produces new knowledge, and is contrasted with co-operative labour which is the direct co-operation of living individuals in a normal material production process. He also observes that 'the trail-blazers generally go bankrupt' while 'the most worthless and miserable sort of money-capitalists . . . draw the greatest profit out of all new developments of the universal labour of the human spirit' (p. 103).

Chapter 6. The effect of price fluctuations

Section 1. Fluctuations in the price of raw materials

If the volume and rate of surplus-value remain constant, a change in the price of raw materials will alter the constant capital required and hence cause an inverse change in the rate of profit. Foreign trade may raise the rate of profit by making cheap raw materials available. Marx also notes that the *amount* of profit may change when the price of raw material changes, because of the difficulty of passing on these changes in the price; if so, the effect on the *rate* of profit would be reinforced. In considering this latter possibility, Marx is temporarily dropping the assumption that prices are proportional to values.

The relative importance of raw material prices rises over time, as labour costs and machinery costs per unit of output fall. Labour costs fall because productivity is rising, while machinery costs fall despite the increased use of machinery because production increases even faster.

Section 2. Appreciation, depreciation, release and tie-up of capital

If the price of means of production increases or decreases, capital already invested in means of production will appreciate or depreciate correspondingly. If the price increases, more capital will be required (tie-up of capital) while if the price decreases capital will be released, since less capital will be required to replace the means of production. (These two effects generally counteract each other; if the price rises, capital appreciates, but the enlarged capital is tied up for as long as prices remain high.)

If the value of labour-power changes, there is no appreciation or depreciation of capital, since labour-power does not transfer its value to the product, but the rate of surplus-value changes. There is, however, a release or tie-up of capital when the price of labour-power changes.

As capitalism develops, the production of organic raw materials tends to lag behind demand, because of natural limits on output. If so, prices rise and induce various adaptations; materials may be shipped from greater distances, production will be stepped up (after a time lag), and substitutes may be used. Nevertheless, price increases will reduce the rate of profit and may provoke a depression, in which prices fall and production is disrupted. The role of agricultural raw material prices in the cycle is rather similar to the role of wages; both tend to rise in periods of prosperity, causing a fall in the rate of profit and a depression which brings prices and wages back down again.

Section 3. General illustration. The cotton crisis of 1861–5

The American civil war of 1861–5 interrupted supplies of cotton, drove up the price, and caused a crisis in the cotton industry in England. Marx goes through the story as an illustration of his analysis of the effects of price fluctuations.

Chapter 7. Supplementary remarks

Profit appears (on a superficial view) to be independent of surplus-value, firstly because it seems to arise in circulation (according to Marx it is created in production and only realized as money in circulation), and secondly because the rate or profit depends on the efficiency with which constant capital is used and on the price of means of production as well as on the rate of surplus-value.

Marx also throws in a criticism of Rodbertus, who had argued that the rate of profit was independent of the magnitude of capital since a change in capital invested would correspond to an equal change in profit. According to Marx's analysis this is true in some particular cases but not in general.

PART 2

Conversion of profit into average profit

The whole analysis of *Capital*, so far, has been based on the assumption that goods exchange at prices proportional to values. Now, at last, Marx analyses how prices are actually formed in the market by competition between capitals. It is hard to overstate the importance of the analysis of 'the transformation of values into prices of production', since it is the key link that connects the abstract theory of surplus-value to the actual day to day working of a capitalist economy.

Competition between capitals tends to equalize profit rates between different industries. A capitalist with a given sum of money to invest will seek to get the highest profit on it that is possible. As a result, capital flows out of industries with low profit rates and into those where profits are high. An inflow of capital into a particular industry increases supply and forces down prices and profits, while an outflow has the opposite result. There is a tendency towards a single *general rate of profit* in all industries, with prices tending towards *prices of production* which are just enough, for each commodity, to yield the general rate of profit on capital invested in producing that commodity.

Prices of production are not, in general, proportional to values, since prices proportional to values would not yield equal profit rates in different industries with different compositions of capital. What Marx has to do is to show how prices of production are related to values. He argues that some prices rise above value while some fall below, but that this merely *redistributes* surplus-value between different capitalists. The *existence* of profit is explained by the theory of surplus-value developed in volume one.

Chapter 8. Different compositions of capitals in different branches of production and resulting differences in rates of profit

Marx has shown, in the previous part, that the rate of profit can vary even if the rate of surplus-value is constant. He now assumes that the rate of surplus-value is the same in different branches of industry within a single country. Competition in the market for labour-power tends to equalize wages and hours of work (and hence the rate of surplus-value). Local barriers to equalization exist, but they tend to break down with the advance of capitalist production.

With the rate of surplus-value given, the amount of surplus-value generated by any capital is directly proportional to the living labour that it sets in motion. With prices proportional to values, the rate of profit depends on the surplus-value generated relative to the total capital advanced, so rates of profit would only be equal in different industries if the living labour set in motion were proportional to the capital advanced. Marx briefly rehearses the definitions of the technical, value and organic compositions of capital (introduced in volume one, chapter twenty five, section one). Since both the composition of capital and its turnover time differ substantially between different sectors of industry, profit rates would differ if prices were proportional to values.

Chapter 9. Formation of a general rate of profit (average rate of profit) and transformation of the values of commodities into prices of production

Prices, Marx argues, must (tend to) be set at levels which yield equal rates of profit in all branches of production; these prices he calls *prices of production*. As he has shown in the previous chapter, profit rates would not be equalized if goods were sold at their values, so prices of production must differ from values. The problem that he tackles next is the relation between prices of production and values; the way prices are actually set in the market is postponed to the next chapter.

He sets up an example with five branches of industry which are taken to represent the way in which the total social capital is distributed between different industries. The rate of surplus-value is assumed to be the same in all industries. Marx also announces that he will assume a turnover time of one year in all industries, although he immediately varies this assumption, in his example, by introducing a distinction between the fixed capital advanced and the value transferred to the cost-price of each commodity by the wearing out of the fixed capital. The value-composition of capital differs between industries, so the rate of profit would differ (as shown in Marx's first table) if products were sold at their values.

The next step is to compute the total surplus-value, and the total capital advanced, for all (five) capitals taken together, and to divide the former by the latter to get an average rate of profit. In the example, total surplus-value is 110 and total capital is 500, so the average rate of profit is 22%. Marx now assumes that each capital must get its share of surplus-value, so that it gets a profit rate equal to the average rate. The price of production of each commodity is calculated by taking its cost-price and adding a profit margin equal to the average profit rate multiplied by the capital advanced. In the example, if a capital of 100 produces commodities with a cost-price of 70, their price of production is 70 (cost-price) plus 22 (profit margin to yield 22 per cent on a capital of 100) making 92 (this is line one of Marx's third table), and so on.

Marx sums up the results: 'different rates of profit are equalized by competition to a single general rate of profit . . . So far as profits are concerned, the various capitalists are just so many stockholders in a stock company in which the shares of profit are uniformly divided per 100' (p. 156). The redivision of surplus-value provides an objective basis for the class solidarity of capitalists and for the mystified view of profit and of capital in non-Marxist political economy.

Total profit for the whole economy is equal to the total surplus-value generated, and the sum of the prices of production of the whole annual product is equal to its total value. Marx's explanation is somewhat obscure, but the point is simple. Total profit is equal to total surplus-value, because that is how the average rate of profit is calculated. The sum of prices of production is the sum of the cost-prices of all products, plus total profit, while the sum of values is the sum of cost-prices plus total surplus-value, so the two must be equal, given Marx's method of derivation. The theory of surplus-value therefore (according to Marx's argument) explains total profit and the general profit rate.

Variations in turnover time between sectors can also be incorporated (though Marx does not explain the details). A longer turnover time in one sector, compared with others, means that a larger capital is required, and the price of production must be higher to yield average profit on the capital concerned.

There remains a major difficulty with Marx's analysis, which Marx touches on twice but dismisses casually. ('Our present analysis does not necessitate a closer examination of this point' p. 162.) If goods are sold at their prices of production, then the buyers must obviously pay these prices, and Marx is inconsistent in calculating cost-prices in terms of values $(c + v)$ when he is assuming that the goods are sold at prices of production.

Marx himself seems to have regarded the problem as a detail that could be cleared up later, and he may have intended to return to it. Further analysis in fact shows that much more than details are involved. Cost-prices clearly have to be recalculated to allow for the fact that capitalists who sell at prices of production also have to buy at prices of production; costs and prices then have to be determined simultaneously, since each depends on the other. Worse still, the capital advanced must be recalculated, since the profit rate that is equalized by competition is the profit on the money-capital advanced to buy means of production and labour-power, and the capital required depends on actual market *prices*. The whole analysis is now cast adrift, since Marx's procedure rests on the average profit calculated on the *value* of advanced capital.

The upshot is that Marx's approach to the transformation problem must be either abandoned or completely reconstructed, which poses serious questions for the whole system of analysis presented in *Capital*. Value and surplus-value would be wholly metaphysical concepts if they could not be linked to actual prices and profits.

It is not surprising that the transformation problem has been the subject of intense debate.[6] That debate lies outside the scope of this guide. The general consensus now seems to be that Marx's conclusions can be rescued in general terms, though not in detail, provided joint-production and all but the simplest cases of fixed capital are ignored. The difficulty in these cases (which are of great importance in practice) is not so much with the analysis of prices of production, but with the prior question of how to define values in cases of joint-production (two or more different commodities produced by a single process).

Chapter 10. Equalization of the general rate of profit through competition. Market-prices and market-values. Surplus-profit

Prices of production have, so far, only been discussed in the abstract, as the result of a hypothetical equalization of profit rates. Marx now moves on to discuss how a tendency towards prices of production is manifested through competition in the market. He does not by any means present a full analysis of competition or of the formation of market-prices, and what he does say on these issues is not easy to understand because it is not fully worked out. In addition, the chapter has all the marks of a preliminary draft rather than a polished final version.

Marx first runs over some characteristics of prices of production that follow from the analysis of the preceding chapter. Since the general rate of profit is the average over the whole social capital, those spheres of production in which the composition of capital is the same as the social average will have prices of production equal to value, and so on. He then poses the question: how is the equalization of profits brought about?

In common with his classical predecessors, Marx thinks of price determination in terms of a 'normal' price, a 'centre', around which the market-price fluctuates. His main concern is with 'normal' prices, and his discussion of price fluctuations is secondary.

Prices, he says, fluctuate around prices of production rather than values, because commodities are the products of capital. By contrast, if workers owned their own means of production, prices would tend to values.

In such a system, a system of 'simple' commodity production, workers would buy means of production, produce commodities, and exchange them. If goods were exchanged at their values, each worker would be able to pay for the means of production used up (since their value is transferred to the product) and would be left with a net income proportional to the (socially necessary) labour performed. This net income would include what would be 'wages' and 'profit', in a capitalist context, but neither 'profit' nor the 'rate of profit' would be relevant in the absence of capital.

Presumably (Marx is not explicit) prices would tend to values because of migration of workers from one sector to another in search of the highest return for their labour, in the same way as wages are equalized by migration of labour in a capitalist system. The argument is debatable; how would workers migrate into sectors in which abnormally large outlays on means of production are necessary? Since simple commodity production predates developed capitalism, Marx concludes that the values of commodities are 'not only theoretically but also historically *prius* to the prices of production' (p. 174).[7]

Marx next turns to the relation between market-prices and values, abstracting for the time being from the factors that make prices of production deviate from values.

First, the concept of value is defined again. The *individual value* of a particular article is the labour actually used to produce it. Since identical items sold in the same market must command the same price (the buyer is not interested in the particular circumstances in which a particular item was produced), the *market-value* of a commodity is the average amount of labour required to produce an item of that type. If a commodity is produced under various conditions (favourable, normal, unfavourable), 'normal' conditions will represent the average if favourable and unfavourable conditions balance out; if favourable or unfavourable conditions predominate, the average will be altered accordingly. The average must be taken over the mass of the commodity needed to satisfy demand when the commodity is sold at its value. If large quantities are demanded, then the part of production carried out under unfavourable circumstances (crops grown on relatively poor land, for example) may have to be expanded in order to meet the demand, and the value of the commodity will rise accordingly.

Actual market-prices remain to be explained. One of Marx's main purposes was to attack the 'vulgar' economists of the time, who thought that 'demand and supply' provided an adequate explanation of prices. (It was said, though not by Marx, that one could train a parrot to be an economist, by teaching it to repeat 'demand and supply'.) The concepts of 'supply' and 'demand' current at the time were not very clearly defined, and Marx did nothing to clarify them.

The amount of a commodity offered for sale and the amount that consumers are willing to buy both depend on the price of a commodity. Any statement about the relation between supply and demand therefore has to specify the price that is assumed. One must also specify the time period involved in any discussion of the response of production to price changes, since adjustments of production take time. Marx is aware of these facts, but he lacked the technical apparatus to present their consequences clearly.

Modern economists treat 'supply' and 'demand' as functions (in the mathematical sense) representing the relation between quantity and price. Marx does not do so, and a reader familiar with modern supply and demand analysis must beware of misinterpreting Marx. Marx seems to think of 'supply' and 'demand' as actual quantities, which raises the question: what price is assumed? An interpretation that is consistent with at least some of Marx's arguments is that 'supply' and 'demand' are defined as the quantities supplied and demanded when price equals market-value. So, he writes: 'Supply and demand coincide when their mutual proportions are such that the mass of commodities of a definite line of production can be sold at their market-value, neither above nor below it' (p. 185). Other, similar, statements could be interpreted in the same way, but it is not even clear that Marx's concept was as definite as this interpretation suggests.

The interpretation proposed here would justify Marx's notorious insistence that supply and demand do not determine normal prices, but only fluctuations around them. Supply and demand, as defined above, do not determine market-value, since market-value must first be known in order to measure supply and demand. Modern economists would regard supply and demand not as the ultimate determinants of prices, but as the way in which underlying costs of production (on the supply side) and social wants (on the demand side) are translated into market-prices. Given the different conceptions of supply and demand involved, there is no necessary conflict between the two views.

Suppose the supply and demand for a particular commodity do not coincide when price equals value. Then the price must rise above value (if demand exceeds supply) or fall below it (if supply exceeds demand). How does this change in price actually take place? 'If the demand . . . is greater than the supply, one buyer outbids another . . . and so raises the price of the commodity for all of them above the market-value' (p. 190). At the higher price, of course, the amount bought will match the amount offered for sale. (In the language of modern textbooks it would be said that the quantities supplied and demanded had been equated by the change in price.)

The increased price and the corresponding profits will then attract capital into the industry, leading to increased production, which drives the price down again. In a fully capitalist economy prices will tend towards prices of production, not values, since it is above average profit rates that attract investment. This part of the story is straightforward and is the main justification for Marx's assertion that prices tend to prices of production. It does not depend on any particular definition of 'supply' or 'demand'. If the price falls below the price of production, the process is reversed, with an outflow of capital to more profitable lines of production. There is, of course, only a *tendency* towards equalization of profits; it takes time for capital to move from one industry to another, and new disturbances arise in the meantime. Market-prices fluctuate around prices of production.

At the end of the chapter Marx introduces another essential concept. Any producer who enjoys more favourable conditions of production than the average will have lower costs than his rivals and will make a *surplus-profit*, a profit above the average. The concept of surplus-profit is the key to Marx's analysis of rent (in part six, below).

Chapter 11. Effects of general wage fluctuations on prices of production

With the help of a numerical example, Marx works out the effect on prices of production of a general increase or decrease of (real) wages. For the total social capital, and consequently for a capital of average composition, the price of production is unchanged when wages rise. Cost-price rises, but surplus-value and hence profit falls by the same amount. For a capital with a lower than average organic composition, wages are a relatively large part of cost-price, so the price of production rises when wages rise. Conversely, where the organic composition is relatively high, the fall in profits outweighs the rise in costs and the price of production falls. For a wage reduction, the reverse results hold. It is not clear what units of measurement Marx is calculating prices in; if prices are measured in money terms (in terms of the money commodity, say gold), then prices will also be affected by changes in the price of production of gold.

Chapter 12. Supplementary remarks

Section 1. Causes implying a change in the price of production

A (permanent) change in the general rate of profit can only occur through a change in the rate of surplus-value or a change in the average composition or turnover of capital. These changes accompany changes in the productivity of labour. Alternatively, prices of production will change if cost-prices change, again as a result of a change in the productivity of labour. Prices of production can only change, therefore, if there is a change in the productivity of labour and hence in the values of commodities. (This argument neglects general wage changes, discussed in the previous chapter.)

Section 2. Price of production of commodities of average composition

Marx now returns to the possibility that the cost-price of a commodity may deviate from $c + v$ because of a difference between price and value in the commodities that make up constant capital or in those consumed by workers. He argues that the price of production of a capital of average composition will still not be affected by a wage change. Since he does not allow for the possible change in cost-price that might result from a wage change (because of the resulting change in the price of means of production or of necessities), his argument is invalid.

Section 3. The capitalist's grounds for compensation

The establishment of a general rate of profit conceals the origin of surplus-value. 'Thus everything appears reversed in competition' (p. 205, emphasis removed). Once a general rate of profit is established, it enters the calculations of capitalists. They seem to be entitled to receive profit at the average rate, and factors such as a high organic composition of capital, slow turnover, or high risks, which reduce the overall profit rate, appear to be the cause of profits, rather than a hindrance to profit.

PART 3

The law of the tendency of the rate of profit to fall

Chapter 13. The law as such

Economists in Marx's time generally believed that there was a tendency for the rate of profit to fall. Marx agreed, but proposed a new explanation. He also disagreed with his predecessors about the consequences of falling profits. He expected the eventual collapse and overthrow of capitalism, where they predicted an eventual 'stationary state' in which capitalist institutions would remain intact.

Marx's 'law' of the tendency of the rate of profit to fall has stimulated much debate.[8] In theoretical terms, the problem is that Marx described a 'tendency' together with a number of 'counteracting influences' that have the opposite effect. He gives no good reason to expect the 'tendency' to prevail over the 'counteracting influences'. There has, in practice, been no consistent falling trend in profit rates.

The meat of Marx's argument is contained in the first few pages of the chapter. Following the analysis of chapter three, the rate of profit is equal to $s'v/C$, where s' is the rate of surplus-value, v is the annual flow of variable capital advances (so $s'v$ is annual surplus-value) and C is total capital advanced. The general rate of profit is determined by the average for the total social capital (as Marx has argued in chapter nine), so v and C are to be interpreted as totals for the whole economy. At this stage, an annual turnover is assumed, so v/C can be written as $v/(c + v)$. It will decrease if the value composition of capital, c/v increases.

If s', the rate of surplus-value, is constant, a decrease in v/C resulting from an increase in the value composition of capital would mean a fall in the rate of profit. So much is simple arithmetic. Marx also assumes that there is no change in the value of the commodities used as means of production, and no change in the value of labour-power, so that an increase in the technical composition of capital (and hence in the organic composition, which is a measure of changes in the technical composition) necessarily and directly increases the value composition.

Given these assumptions, an increase in the technical composition of capital necessarily leads to a fall in the rate of profit. Marx asserts that the technical composition of capital rises as productivity rises, since each worker processes a greater volume of raw materials, using a greater quantity of equipment.

He concludes that: 'The progressive tendency of the general rate of profit to fall is, therefore, just *an expression peculiar to the capitalist mode of production* of the progressive development of the social productivity of labour . . . it is thereby proved a logical necessity that in its development the general average rate of surplus-value must express itself in a falling general rate of profit' (p. 209, emphasis in original).

It is easy to see why this extraordinarily strong statement has come under attack. The 'countertendencies' that are being ignored are not all simply random disturbances that can reasonably be neglected, but are themselves direct results of increasing productivity. It is logically inconsistent to hold both the rate of surplus-value and the value of labour-power constant when productivity is increasing; one or the other must change. Similarly, rising productivity must entail a fall in the value of commodities used as means of production.

Marx argues, in passing, that the same principle can explain why profit rates should be higher in underdeveloped than in advanced countries, though differences in the rate of surplus-value should also be taken into account.

The argument is then restated. The mass of living labour (the source of surplus-value) declines *relative* to the mass of labour embodied in means of production. The absolute amount of living labour employed will normally expand, and so will the mass of surplus-value and of profit, but advanced capital increases more rapidly still, so the *rate* of profit may fall while the *mass* of profit rises.

Marx emphasizes that his theory is independent of the division of surplus-value into various categories (profit, interest, rent). In this he differs from Ricardo, who explained the falling rate of profit in terms of an increasing share of rent. He also criticizes those who explain falling profits as being the result of increasing competition or of falling prices caused by expanded supply. Prices are a result, and not a cause, since prices of production are determined by cost-price plus profit. This shaft is aimed at Smith and his followers.

A section on turnover was inserted by Engels. In the equation $p' = s'v/C$, v is the *annual flow* of variable capital, while C is the *initial capital* advanced. A reduction in turnover time will raise the rate of profit by reducing C relative to v. Since Marx argued (in volume two) that the turnover time of circulating capital tends to fall, this is another counteracting influence, not mentioned in chapter fourteen. On the other hand, an increase in the importance of fixed capital will lengthen turnover time and reduce the profit rate.

Chapter 14. Counteracting influences

Having explained why the rate of profit should fall, Marx now has to explain why it had not in fact fallen as rapidly as might have been expected, so he introduces a number of counteracting influences.

Section 1. Increasing intensity of exploitation

An increase in the productivity of labour tends to raise the rate of surplus-value (relative surplus-value) as well as the organic composition of capital. Marx asserts that the latter tendency dominates in the long run, so that increases in the productivity of labour are among 'the factors that check the fall of the rate of profit, but that always hasten its fall in the last analysis' (p. 228).

An argument that is hinted at in several places, notably in chapter fifteen (below) runs as follows: suppose relative surplus-value were to proceed so far that necessary labour was reduced almost to zero, with all but an infinitesimal fraction of new value accruing to capital as profit. If the ratio of living labour to capital advanced were then to fall, the rate of profit would fall, because living labour is the source of new value which is all, by assumption, profit. Of course, if labour-power were that cheap, capitalists would have no incentive to spend on constant capital to save labour.

Marx also mentions lengthening of the working-day and intensification of labour, which raise the rate of profit, but which are both subject to inherent limits.

Section 2. Depression of wages below the value of labour-power

Depression of wages is mentioned and dismissed. It is not relevant to the theory at this stage, though it is significant in practice.

Section 3. Cheapening of elements of constant capital

Means of production are cheapened by increases in the productivity of labour, and this tends to offset the increase in the mass of means of production used. 'In isolated cases the mass of the elements of constant capital may even increase, while its value remains the same, or falls' (p. 231). A main line of criticism of Marx's theory has focussed on the possibility that such cases may not be 'isolated'; they may even be the rule.

Section 4. Relative overpopulation

Increases in productivity make workers redundant and force down wages, checking the tendency to substitute means of production for labour, and also encouraging the creation of new labour intensive industries that reduce the average composition of capital.

Section 5. Foreign trade

Foreign trade makes it possible to buy (some) necessities of life more cheaply than they could be produced at home, raising the rate of surplus-value, and also to buy (some) means of production cheap, reducing the value composition of capital. From both angles, foreign trade raises the rate of profit.

Capitals invested in foreign trade can realize a high rate of profit, and Marx presents a rather inconclusive discussion of whether these profits help to raise the general rate of profit. This paragraph is often quoted in the context of Marxist discussions of colonialism and imperialism, though it is doubtful whether any conclusions can safely be drawn from it.

Section 6. The increase of stock capital

Some enterprises, such as railways, are organised as joint-stock companies (corporations). Marx argues that these yield only low rates of profit, since their dividends need only match the rate of interest, which is lower than the general rate of profit. Since these capitals make less than average profit, they leave more for the rest. Modern readers may be surprised at the idea that large corporations are relatively unprofitable.

Chapter 15. Exposition of the internal contradictions of the law

Section 1. General

A fall in the rate of profit 'breeds overproduction, speculation, crises, and surplus-capital alongside surplus-population' (p. 237). It is a barrier to the further development of capitalism nd poses severe problems for economists who see no alteɪ ative to capitalism.

Ricardo explained a falling rate of profit as the result of a rising share of rent. Marx's explanation involves a falling ratio of surplus-value (industrial profit plus interest plus rent) to capital, so it is possible, indeed likely, that both profit and rent may fall relative to total capital.

Surplus-value (and therefore profit) must be realized by the sale of the product. Realization is constrained by 'consumer power based on antagonistic conditions of distribution, which reduce the consumption of the bulk of society to a minimum varying within more or less narrow limits' (p. 239). This hint is not developed further.

Section 2. Conflict between expansion of production

The capitalist mode of production tends to develop the forces of production, but in so doing it promotes a falling rate of profit, crisis and the depreciation of existing capital, and thus comes into conflict with its own limited purpose, the self-expansion of capital.

Section 3. Excess capital and excess population

'Absolute overproduction of capital' occurs when an increase in capital could not extract any more surplus-value from the existing working population. This would only occur if the population were fully employed already, in which case any further accumulation would increase the demand for labour-power above the supply, drive up wages and reduce the rate of surplus-value. This barrier to capitalist accumulation has, of course, nothing to do with the law of the tendency of the rate of profit to fall, since it concerns a change in the rate of surplus-value and not in the composition of capital.

Falling profits precipitate a crisis and a fierce competitive struggle for markets. (Some economists, notably Smith, had explained a falling rate of profit as the result of competition; Marx reverses the causality.) Prices fall, capital depreciates, the chain of payments is broken and the credit system disrupted. However, the crisis creates the conditions for its own resolution. Wages fall, and new methods of production are brought into use that raise productivity and cheapen the elements of constant capital. The stage is set for subsequent expansion and for a repetition of the cycle. The law of the tendency of the rate of profit to fall plays little part in this story, which, brief as it is, is one of the most complete accounts of the cyclical process to be found in Marx's work.

Section 4. Supplementary remarks

Marx finishes the discussion of the falling rate of profit with some rather disconnected remarks. Some sectors advance more slowly than others. The value of fixed capital increases at a slower rate than productivity. Capitalists do not voluntarily introduce methods of production that lower the rate of profit; the innovator makes a higher profit, a super-profit, that is competed away as others copy. (The argument of the last sentence does not demonstrate that the profit rate will be lower once profits are equalized on the new basis; what it shows is that the temporary profits made by innovators are irrelevant to the long-run trend in the general rate.)

PART 4

Conversion of commodity-capital and money-capital into commercial capital and money-dealing capital (merchant's capital)

According to Marx, the source of surplus-value, and hence of profit, is to be found in capitalist production, not in exchange. He still has to explain the profits received by merchants, whose capital (*commercial capital*)does not function in production at all. This form of capital existed before capitalist production and therefore before industrial capital. Some economists treated it as the prototypical form of capital; Marx disagrees.

Chapter 16. Commercial capital

The circuit of capital involves both production and circulation; a part of the total social capital is always in the form of commodities, or of money, in the sphere of circulation. Merchants buy goods for resale, without performing any production, so their capital, *commercial capital* or *merchant's capital*, is a part of the capital of circulation.

When a merchant buys from an industrial capitalist, the industrialist completes the sale of his product, and is able to reconvert the proceeds into productive capital immediately, while the merchant takes over the function of selling. Commercial capital is therefore a specialized fraction of industrial capital, performing a specialized function and split off as an independent fraction of the total capital. The industrial capitalist needs less capital, since his turnover is shortened, and the merchant instead of the industrialist advances the capital required during the time of circulation.

No value is produced in circulation (which must not be confused with transport or other productive activities), so merchant's capital produces no value. It may indirectly promote the production of surplus-value in industry by speeding circulation and by enlarging the market and thus promoting large scale production, but that is irrelevant to the explanation of commercial profit.

Chapter 17. Commercial profit

Commercial capital produces no value, but must receive profit at the same general rate on capital invested as any other capital. If it did not, there would be migration of capital into or out of commercial activities until profit rates were equalized.

Suppose industrial capitalists carried out all commercial operations themselves. Part of their capital would be tied up in circulation, and there would be costs in circulation (wages of salesmen, warehouses, etc.). In calculating average profit, capital tied up in circulation must be counted as part of total capital, and costs of circulation must be subtracted from surplus-value. Average profit, obviously, comes out lower than it would do if selling were costless and took no time.

Now suppose that commercial capital takes over the function of selling. Merchants, too, must cover their costs and receive profit at the general rate, so nothing essential is changed, except that commercial costs may be lower since merchants reap economies in carrying out their specialized functions. Industrial capitalists sell at a price that yields average profit to them, and merchants sell at the full price of production. Commercial wage-workers receive a wage determined by the value of labour-power, just as industrial workers do, though they produce no value.

The general rate of profit is a sharing-out of the surplus-value generated in production; merchant's capital gets its share. Commercial profit, does, of course, appear as a difference between buying and selling prices, but that is the way profit is distributed, not how it is generated in the first place.

Chapter 18. The turnover of merchant's capital. Prices

A crisis frequently manifests itself first in wholesale trade. Stocks build up in merchants' hands until banks press for repayment of loans, forced sales result, and the crisis comes out in the open.

Monopoly apart, the merchant does not determine his own selling price and profit; they are determined through competition by the general rate of profit. Marx stresses this point to combat the idea that profits are explained by the adding of a profit margin onto the cost of goods.

A reduction in the turnover time of industrial capital allows a given capital to produce more surplus-value in a given time, and so raises the general rate of profit. A reduction in the turnover time of merchant's capital reduces the part of the total social capital tied up unproductively in circulation, so it too raises the general rate of profit.

Chapter 19. Money-dealing capital

Just as commercial capital performs specialized functions in buying and selling, so the technical functions of handling money, such as foreign exchange transactions, safekeeping, record keeping, the making of payments, and so on, can be delegated to a specialized fraction of capital, which will receive its due share of profit. Marx keeps these *money-dealing* functions separate from the credit system, for analytical clarity; in practice, banks carry out money-dealing activities and also act as intermediaries in borrowing and lending.

Chapter 20. Historical facts about merchant's capital

Commodity exchange and merchant's capital both existed before the development of capitalist production. Marx makes a clear distinction between simple commodity exchange on the one hand and fully capitalist production, involving wage-labour, on the other. In this he differs from writers (including some Marxists) who identify the rise of commerce with the rise of capitalism.

In a fully capitalist system, merchant's capital takes its share in surplus-value in the way Marx has analysed. Other systems of production, however, may produce surplus products that can be traded, and wherever there is trade there is scope for merchants to act as middlemen. Merchant's capital plays a dominant role precisely in those areas or periods of history in which capitalist production is least developed. In these cases the profits of trade are not determined by any equalization of profit rates, and may include a large element of cheating and outright piracy.

The development of the world-market did play an essential role in the emergence of capitalism, but only where other conditions were ripe. In particular, the crucial ingredient in primitive accumulation was the creation of a proletariat by the separation of producers from the means of production (see volume one, part eight). Where social structures were such that this development did not take place (Marx cites India and China as particular examples), commerce effected at most a slow disintegration of pre-existing modes of production.

In the early stages of capitalist development, merchants exercised control over small producers, but this system was only a stepping stone to mature capitalism, which requires that the capitalist producer establish his independence. Merchant capital then becomes the servant of industrial capital, not its master.

Division of profit into interest and profit of enterprise. Interest-bearing capital

Marx's discussion of interest-bearing capital falls into two parts (though the division is not entirely clear cut). First, Marx is concerned with interest as a category of income, and his main purpose is to emphasize that it is created by a division of profit (and hence of surplus-value) between interest and profit of enterprise. Theories of interest cannot explain profits.

Second, Marx analyses the credit system and the banking system, the relation of credit to money and to capital, and the monetary aspect of economic crises. His discussion of these topics was left in a very unfinished state. Marx's method of work was to start off with a mass of quotations from various sources which he worked over and criticized until, in his final polished work, the quotations have either been eliminated or have been reduced to a clearly secondary role as supporting evidence. In some of the chapters on credit he never got beyond the first stage, and it is even difficult, in some cases, to tell whether Marx quoted a particular extract in order to agree or to disagree with it.

Chapter 21. Interest-bearing capital

In a capitalist system, money can be advanced as capital to make a profit. An individual who owns a sum of money can lend it, hand the use of it over for a period of time, to another who can then use it to make a profit. Interest is payment for the use of a sum of money, and arises because, in a capitalist framework, money has the use-value of producing a profit.

Money lent in this way becomes capital, and Marx calls it *interest-bearing capital* or *money-capital*. The terminology can be confusing; in Marx's analysis so far, the term 'money-capital' has been used to describe a transient phase in the circuit of capital; money-capital is transformed into productive-capital, and so on. Here the word is used in a quite different sense, and it would be clearer if Marx had stuck rigidly to the term 'interest-bearing capital'. When money is lent at interest it passes out of the hands of the lender, who then has only a claim to interest and to repayment. (Marx later introduces the term 'fictitious capital' to describe these claims.) To the borrower, the borrowed money becomes money-capital and is then transformed into productive capital. Marx often refers to the lender as a 'money-capitalist'.

Interest is a part of profit, determined by the supply of, and demand for, loans. There is, according to Marx, no 'natural' rate of interest governed by any more fundamental principle.

Chapter 22. Division of profit. Rate of interest. Natural rate of interest

Since interest is a part of profit, the normal upper limit of the rate of interest is set by the rate of profit (after subtracting wages of superintendance, which will be discussed below). The minimum 'is altogether indeterminable' (p. 351), so interest might fall to any level provided it is fractionally above zero.

If the relation of interest to profit were fixed, the interest rate would rise and fall with the profit rate. The tendency of the profit rate to fall would therefore mean that the interest rate would tend to fall with it. The interest rate tends to fall even more, because of the increasing wealth of a class of idle money-capitalists, and also because of the development of the credit system, which mobilizes idle hoards of money, both factors which increase the supply of interest-bearing capital. During the cycle, interest rates stay low during the period of prosperity but rise abruptly in the crisis, as demands emerge for cash at any price to meet payments that are due. The credit system and its relation to crises will be discussed at greater length later.

Marx insists, again, that there is no natural rate of interest. Interest rates are determined by demand and supply, so 'the determination is accidental, purely empirical, and only pedantry or fantasy would seek to represent this accident as a necessity' (p. 356). This is one of Marx's strongest dismissals of demand and supply; it raises difficult questions as to what Marx meant by 'accident' and 'necessity'. In one sense, presumably, nothing is accidental, everything has a cause, and Marx himself advances various explanations of the trend of demand and supply (see above). What Marx must mean here is that the magnitudes of demand and supply cannot be linked to any more fundamental features of capitalism.

Chapter 23. Interest and profit of enterprise

If a capitalist operates entirely with borrowed money, interest takes part of the profit, and is a return to the mere ownership of capital, while the remainder, which Marx calls *profit of enterprise*, is a return to the active performance of the functions of a capitalist. Even a capitalist who operates with his own money can mentally divide his profit into two parts; the part he could get by merely lending out his money (interest) and the extra that accrues to him as an active capitalist (profit of enterprise).

The division of profit into two parts does not in any way explain why any profit exists to be divided; according to Marx, of course, profit derives from surplus-value and hence from exploitation.

Since profit of enterprise is a return to the actual work of being an active capitalist, it appears to be a wage, the wages of superintendence. The work of superintendence has two aspects. Co-ordination is necessary in any system, but the antagonistic character of a class society causes additional needs for superintendence. Individuals may be employed as managers and paid wages. In co-operative factories (owned by the workers), managers are employed to carry out the function of co-ordination.

Wages of superintendence, presumably, do not account for all of profit of enterprise. If they did, and if they were determined in the same way as the wages of other kinds of skilled labour-power, there would be a natural rate of interest: profit minus wages of superintendance. Marx is not clear on this point.

Chapter 24. Externalization of the relations of capital in the form of interest-bearing capital

Interest-bearing capital is the most mysterious and fetishized form of capital. It seems as if a sum of money has the inherent property of producing more money. 'Vulgar economy' takes interest-bearing capital as the typical form of capital, leading to fantasies such as that of Dr Price, who calculated how much a shilling put out at compound interest in the year zero would have been worth by the time he wrote.

Chapter 25. Credit and fictitious capital

As Marx has already stated (briefly) in volume one, commodity exchange commonly operates on credit; the seller agrees to accept delayed payment. Marx takes the 'bill of exchange' to be the typical form of credit; it is a written promise to pay, which in Marx's time was commonly passed on as if it were money. Bills can also be 'discounted' by banks who pay the holder immediately (but pay less than the face value, subtracting interest; hence the interest rate may be called a 'discount rate') and collect when the bill falls due.

Banks carry out technical operations connected with money, and they also manage interest-bearing capital. In addition, reserve-funds and temporarily idle money holdings of all sorts are deposited in banks, and small sums of money are thus mobilized by being collected together into sums large enough to serve as capital. Banks are able to hold a minimum of idle reserves, and to lend the rest of the money deposited with them, by discounting bills and making advances (loans). Bank notes issued by private banks are simply drafts on the banker, though they may circulate as money. The institutional framework of banking and of credit in Marx's time may well be unfamiliar to modern readers; it is discussed in the introduction, above, p. 17.

Fictitious capital, which appears in the chapter title, is not in fact defined until chapter twenty-nine. Much of the chapter is taken up with descriptive quotations from various authors.

Chapter 26. Accumulation of money-capital. Its influence on the interest rate

Marx next pursues his analysis of the determination of interest rates by the demand for, and supply of, loans, in the rather obscure form of commentaries on the evidence given by Norman and by Overstone to parliamentary enquiries. The main point seems to be that a capitalist may seek to borrow in order to obtain capital to expand his operations, or he may borrow in order to get capital in the form of money at a time when he is short of cash (generally in a crisis). These two cases must presumably be distinguished because borrowers who intend to expand their operations will only borrow if the interest rate is less than the profit rate they can expect, while interest on 'distress borrowing' is not limited in the same way. In the first case, borrowing is directly linked to an expansion of production, and in the second case it is not. Marx returns to this issue later. Norman and Overstone are also criticized for various confusions which have little to do with the point at issue.

Another issue, of great practical importance at the time, concerns the effect of flows of money across national boundaries. A bad harvest would lead to an import of grain paid for by an outflow of gold from the reserves of the Bank of England. The Bank of England would react by cutting back its lending in order to restore its reserves, and the interest rate would rise because of the reduced supply of loans. This sort of influence on interest rates must be distinguished from the conditions of reproduction of real productive capital.

Chapter 27. The role of credit in capitalist production

Marx now digresses to make some general comments on credit and on joint-stock companies. Credit contributes to the equalization of profit rates, by expediting the flow of capital between different sectors, and also reduces costs by reducing the extent to which money is tied up in circulation.

The formation of joint-stock companies seemed to Marx to be confirmation of his analysis of capitalism. The separation of the ownership of capital from its use is 'the abolition of the capitalist mode of production within the capitalist mode of production itself, and hence . . . a mere phase of transition to a new form of production' (p. 429). It permits massive centralization of capital and hence socialization of production, and at the same time reveals the parasitic role of the capitalist as mere owner. Engels added a note on the further development of the joint-stock form, on cartelization, monopoly and overproduction. These ideas were developed much later in the work of Hilferding, Bukharin and Lenin, in the early twentieth century. In a passing remark, Marx refers to workers' co-operatives as the beginnings of a new social order.

Chapter 28. Medium of circulation and capital; views of Tooke and Fullarton

After the brief but thought-provoking digression on joint-stock companies, Marx returns to the workings of the financial system in his own time, and to contemporary debates. Tooke, he says, confused money as a medium of circulation with money-capital and with interest-bearing capital.

Fullarton got nearer to the point, by making a distinction between a need for additional money in circulation (in a period of prosperity) and a demand for capital on loan (in a crisis). Marx argues that what happens in a crisis is not an increase in the demand for loans, but an increased difficulty in satisfying the demand, a decrease in supply. The main point of the discussion is to reiterate the distinction between a shortage of capital in general and a shortage of money capital, of cash, caused by a difficulty of realizing commodity-capital. In a crisis or depression, productive capital and commodity-capital are not lacking; the problem is that commodities cannot be sold.

Chapter 29. Component parts of bank capital

Marx next discusses the capital of banks, and launches into a digression which is best dealt with first. Once interest-bearing capital is well established, any claim to a regular revenue comes to be thought of as if it were itself a capital, which Marx calls *fictitious capital*. The national debt is an example; money has been lent to the state and spent, so that no capital remains. A bondholder who lent £100 (say) at 5 per cent has a claim to interest of £5 annually, and regards his bond as a capital of £100. The bond can be resold to another individual, at a price that depends on market conditions. Even where a paper asset represents a claim on the profits of a real capital, such as a railway, the bond itself is fictitious capital, since the real capital consists of rails, locomotives, and so on.

Marx adds a sideswipe at those who treat labour-power as a capital owned by the worker. The worker has to work for his wages, unlike the capitalist, and cannot sell his 'capital' outright.

A bank has part of its capital (it might be better to say, the capital it controls) invested in interest-bearing paper (in fictitious capital), a part in discounted bills, and a part in cash reserves. Money deposited with the bank is re-lent (normally, in Marx's time, by discounting bills) and the money thus lent out may be redeposited and lent out again. A multiple superstructure of credit can be built up on a limited basis of actual cash.

Individual deposits are constantly withdrawn and redeposited. Discounted bills fall due and are repaid to the bank, and the bank discounts fresh bills. These transactions all tend to offset each other, so that reserves stay relatively constant.

Chapter 30. Money-capital and real capital I

Marx now turns to a question that has already been touched on. To what extent does an abundance or scarcity of loanable money-capital, as reflected in movements of interest rates, reflect an abundance or scarcity of real (industrial) capital? As Marx has shown, many writers confused the two, arguing that a high interest rate reflected a scarcity, and a low rate, an abundance, of 'capital'. The focus of Marx's analysis is on movements in interest rates over the course of the industrial cycle, and his discussion contains many interesting asides on the cycle itself.

The first step is to clear some ground and define the problem more clearly. The issue is confused by the existence of masses of fictitious capital, bonds and other paper assets which represent past loans, not current borrowing and lending. It is only the supply and demand of currently available loanable funds, primarily channelled through banks, that counts.

Abstracting even from bank credit, there remains commercial credit given by one industrial or commercial capitalist to another by deferring payment for commodities. Credit of this sort automatically expands and contracts with the movements of real production; the expansion of credit in periods of prosperity does not in any way indicate a superabundance of idle capital.

In a crisis, circulation is blocked, confidence is shaken, sellers become unwilling to extend credit and buyers become unable to meet their obligations when bills fall due. The volume of credit falls and loanable money-capital becomes scarce, while productive-capital is superabundant, i.e. it cannot all function productively, and is immobilized in the form of stocks of unsaleable commodities. The only case where there is a real lack of productive capital is when there is a crop failure, or a similar failure of real reproduction.

If only industrial capitalists and workers existed (other groups will be brought into the story later), a crisis could only arise because of a disproportion between branches, or a disproportion between production and demand. A deficiency of demand does not mean a lack of real needs. 'The ultimate reason for all real crises always remains the poverty and restricted consumption of the masses' (p. 472). This oft-quoted sentence must be taken in conjunction with Marx's statements elsewhere that high, not low, wages immediately precede a crisis.

Bank credit can sustain an illusion of smooth reproduction right up to the eve of the crisis, so the crash comes as a surprise and appears to be the result of the financial collapse instead of its cause.

Now banks can be added to the story. They advance credit, draw on the savings of unproductive classes and mobilize the reserve-funds of active capitalists. In the depression that follows a crisis, banks have idle loanable capital which can find no outlet, given the contraction of reproduction, so interest rates are low. In the recovery, commercial credit expands, confidence is high, and interest rates remain low, the only case in which an abundance of loanable capital coincides with an expansion of the reproduction of real capital. As expansion continues, fixed investment picks up, firms draw on bank credit for expansion, speculative schemes emerge, and the interest rate starts to rise again.

The industrial cycle constantly reproduces itself. Engels adds a note here, which looks forward to later theories of imperialism. He describes the expansion of the world-market, the growth of monopoly and of national protective tariffs.

The chapter ends with some further notes on the cycle. As prices rise in a boom, the consuming power of unproductive classes (those who receive fixed money incomes) declines. It is not clear whether Marx regards this as a contributing factor in the downturn.

Crises are transmitted internationally; the cycle is a phenomenon of the world-market and is not confined to any one country. An outflow of gold from any particular country, however, is a symptom not a cause; writers of the time placed undue emphasis on gold movements.

Chapter 31. Money-capital and real capital II

Marx now turns his attention to the sources of loanable money-capital.

Section 1. Transformation of money into loan capital

The development of banking techniques economizes on money reserve-funds and mobilizes quantities of money to be lent out. This increased supply of loan capital is quite distinct from any accumulation of productive capital. Loan capital must also be distinguished from money in circulation; the same money can be lent, used in transactions, redeposited in banks and lent out again.

In passing, Marx comments that the maximum level of real production before a crisis is the starting point for the next prosperity, which rises to a new peak, and so on.

Section 2. Transformation of capital or revenue into money that is transformed into loan capital

As the financial system develops, a class of money-lending capitalists grows; their growing wealth is always in money form and is available for lending. In crises, the market-price of paper assets (bills, etc.) falls, and money-capitalists buy up these assets, so an increasing fraction of wealth comes into their hands.

The profits of active capitalists are accumulated as money waiting to be advanced as productive-capital or spent on consumption, and these sums, too, become available for lending.

Chapter 32. Money-capital and real capital III

The discussion of money-capital and real capital is rounded off with a number of rather disconnected points, mainly serving to emphasize the distinction between the two. Crises apart, a long period of high interest rates does indicate high profits on real capital, but high interest rates in themselves tend to reduce profit of enterprise. Favourable conditions for profits, then, may raise the demand for money-capital and for productive capital. Increased real investment will raise the demand for labour-power and tend to raise wages. This correlation between high wages and high interest rates does not, of course, mean that high wages are the cause of high profits or of high interest rates.

Chapter 33. The medium of circulation in the credit system

Marx's discussion of credit and circulation was left in a very confused state; Engels, as editor, rearranged it as best he could. In any case, systems of payment in England at the time Marx wrote were in a state of transition that was confusing enough in itself. At that date, payments might be made in coin, in bank notes (which were issued by private banks and were convertible into gold), by passing on bills of exchange issued by capitalist firms and guaranteed by banks, or by transferring bank deposits by cheque. This last, which has since become the normal method of payment for all substantial transactions, is not discussed by Marx at all. Modern economists universally treat bank deposits as money; Marx does not.

A number of points emerge from Marx's discussion. The development of the credit system and the improvement of communications speeds up the circulation of money; for example, the volume of bank notes in circulation actually fell from 1844 to 1857 despite a large increase in the scale of business. Convertible notes, Marx argues, can only circulate to the extent that they are needed for transactions; any excess will be returned to the issuing bank. The note circulation expands and contracts with the industrial cycle in response to the needs of circulation. It should be emphasized again that Marx's arguments apply to the institutional framework of the time, and in particular to a monetary system in which bank notes were convertible into gold.

Chapter 34. The currency principle and the English bank legislation of 1844

According to Ricardo (and others) the value of money rises or falls in inverse proportion to the amount of money in circulation; this is the 'quantity theory of money'. A general price increase (a fall in the value of money) is caused by an excessive amount of money in circulation. In a simple open economy, like that of Britain, a price increase would lead to a loss of export markets, an outflow of gold and, assuming gold to be money, a contraction of the money supply, remedying the evil. Problems arise, in this view, when bank notes came into circulation, allowing overexpansion of the money supply, leading to a subsequent crisis. The legislation of 1844 restricted the note issue of the Bank of England so that the limit of the issue was directly linked to the Bank's holdings of gold.

Marx is scornful of the supporters of the Ricardian view, the 'currency school'. In his opinion, which broadly coincides on this issue (only) with the 'banking school' (see the introduction, pp. 10–11 above), convertibility of notes into gold is an adequate safeguard against overissue. The industrial cycle is not caused by expansion of the note issue, which responds passively to the needs of circulation. Restriction of the note issue only exacerbates crises, or would do so if the act of 1844 were not in practice suspended when necessary.

Chapter 35. Precious metal and rate of exchange

Section 1. Movement of the gold reserve

Flows of gold between countries occur for two reasons. Firstly, gold, like any other commodity, is exported from producing areas to areas where there is a demand for it. Secondly, flows of gold between non-gold-producing countries reflect the balance of trade, because gold is the international means of payment. These flows are the result, not the cause, of the industrial cycle. In normal periods, gold is distributed among different countries in proportion to their needs for money circulation.

Section 2. The rate of exchange

As Engels explains, in an interpolation, the exchange rate between national currencies varies with the balance of payments. At the time

Marx was writing, currencies were exchangeable into gold. If England had a balance of payments deficit with Germany (say), more pounds would be offered in exchange for marks (to make payments in Germany) than vice-versa. The pound would depreciate to the point where it would be profitable to obtain gold in England and ship it to Germany. The exchange rate thus serves as an index of the balance of payments.

Marx criticizes the notion that the export of capital is always associated with a drain of gold and a rise in interest rates. If rails are paid for by British capitalists and sent to India to build a railway there, the effect on the balance of payments is just as if they had been installed in Britain. Interest rates need not rise; Marx has already argued that interest rates can stay low through a period of expansion.

Chapter 36. Pre-capitalist relationships

Marx closes the discussion of interest-bearing capital with a historical retrospect, which should be taken together with the discussion of primitive accumulation (volume one, part eight) and the history of merchant's capital (volume three, chapter twenty). Interest-bearing capital (usury), like merchant's capital, predates capitalist production, and has existed in many different systems. Usury and commerce had similar effects on pre-capitalist societies.

Characteristically, the usurer lent to extravagant landlords and to impoverished small producers. Large sums of money were concentrated into the usurer's hands in this way, and interest payments might be high enough to absorb all of the surplus above a bare subsistence for the producer (hence the high interest rates in pre-capitalist societies). Usury developed particularly where payments in money (rents, taxes, etc.) had to be made.

Usury exploited and impoverished the producers without transforming the mode of production; it only played a part in the transition to capitalism where the other prerequisites of capitalist production had emerged. It was parasitic, hence the hatred of usurers in pre-capitalist societies. The development of the modern credit system marked the subordination of interest-bearing capital to the needs of capitalist production. Saint-Simon and other 'socialists' who campaigned against interest were serving the interests of industrial capital, not the working class.

The banking system separates the ownership of capital from its use, and promotes the rational distribution of capital between different activities. It will serve as a lever in the construction of socialism, but only in conjunction with an overthrow of capitalist relations of production.

PART 6

Transformation of surplus-profit into ground-rent

Chapter 37. Introduction

Rent was a major source of income, and played a prominent role in economic theory, in Marx's time. Marx clearly had to show how rent could be explained in terms of his system.

He starts by stressing that he is concerned with rent in a fully capitalist system in which agriculture involves three classes: agricultural wage-labourers, capitalist tenant farmers and landowners. Landownership is 'the monopoly by certain persons over definite portions of the globe' (p. 601). The freedom of individual owners to do what they like with their land is characteristic of the epoch of capitalism. 'Land' here is taken to include agricultural land, building land, water, mines, and so on. In Marx's main exposition, he deals with agricultural land used to produce the principal crop of the country concerned (he refers to the product as 'grain').

Ground-rent is payment to the owner for use of these natural resources. Payments to landowners may also include interest on capital (improvements to the land, buildings, etc.) but these payments are distinct from rent itself. Landowners may also capture part of the average profit that would normally accrue to tenant farmers, or part of the surplus-profit from low agricultural wages, but Marx abstracts from these deviations from the capitalist norm.

The price of land is determined by capitalizing the rent it brings in, since in a capitalist framework ownership of land is simply a source of income. Rent explains the price of land, and not vice-versa. With a 5 per cent interest rate (for example), land that yields a rent of £200 p a is worth £4,000, because £200 is 5 per cent of £4,000. Any asset that brings in £200 p a would be worth £4,000. Since land is a secure and prestigious asset, it may in fact command a relatively high price, i.e. the percentage return on land may be low compared to that on other assets.

Capitalist ground-rent must not be confused with historically earlier forms. All forms of rent arise from surplus-labour, but the issue here is how the landowner can capture part of surplus-value in a capitalist context.

Chapter 38. Differential rent: general remarks

Marx's analysis of *differential rent* (the reason for the term will soon become clear) is based on Ricardo. It differs, as one might expect, in that Marx distinguishes sharply between the natural fertility of the soil, on the one hand, and the social relations that enable the owner to get rent, on the other.

Suppose most factories use steam power, while a smaller number use water power, which is cheaper. Prices of production will be determined by the higher cost producers, while those who use water power will gain a surplus-profit, over and above average profit (see chapter ten). The owners of waterfalls used as power sources can obtain rent equal to this surplus-profit.

Differential rent arises from the conjunction of two factors. Firstly, there is a natural advantage that is only available to some producers, so that it does not enter into the price of production. Secondly, the source of the advantage is monopolized by an individual owner who can claim the surplus-profit as rent, because capitalists will compete for the use of the natural advantage by offering to pay rent. Differential rent arises from differences in costs between producers. The natural force of the waterfall is the basis, not the source of rent; the source of the rent is surplus-labour in the form of surplus-value. Private ownership of land is the means by which an individual captures part of surplus-value as rent.

Chapter 39. First form of differential rent (differential rent I)

The first form of differential rent arises when equal amounts of capital are invested on equal areas of land, but produce different returns because of differences in fertility (or location).

Marx works through an example, with four kinds of land from A (the least fertile) to D (the most fertile). This example, with modifications, is used for the next six chapters. The cost of production on the least fertile land (A), plus average profit, determines the price of production, since A would not be cultivated if it did not yield average profit. All land that is more fertile than this 'marginal' land (not Marx's term) yields rent.

In the analysis of rent at a particular moment, the historical order in which land has been brought into use is not important. If only a little land is needed to meet the demand for agricultural produce, only the most fertile will be used, while if more land is needed, prices will have to rise to make it profitable to farm less fertile land. Marx works through this case (a 'descending sequence'); as the demand for agricultural produce rises, rents rise too, while the general profit rate falls (because grain enters into the cost of reproducing labour-power and an increase in the price of grain will raise the price of labour-power). The demand for agricultural produce depends on population and on the general development of production.

Ricardo, however, interpreted this logical sequence as a historical sequence, and predicted that rents would rise and profits fall as capital was accumulated. Marx stresses that the historical order in which land is brought into cultivation may depend on various factors, and that the relative productiveness of different soils can be altered by the progress of agricultural methods.

The total amount of rent depends on the total acreage, on the difference between the worst land used and the rest, and on the proportions of soil with different levels of fertility.

Chapter 40. Second form of differential rent (differential rent II)

In analysing differential rent I, Marx assumed that equal capitals are invested on equal areas of land. It may, however, pay to invest more capital per acre on fertile land, raising output per acre, surplus-profit and rent. The extra rent is differential rent II. Prices of production are still determined on the least fertile (zero rent) land.

Again there is a rather confusing discussion of the order in which different land is taken into cultivation and different investments made. Most nineteenth-century economists failed to distinguish clearly between the process of development of agriculture as it had happened historically, on the one hand, and the comparison of the returns to different pieces of land and to different scales of investment at a given date, on the other. Marx does separate the two, but found it difficult to escape from the conventional way of presenting the analysis.

Chapter 41. Differential rent II – first case: constant price of production

Marx now works through various (unnecessarily elaborate) examples. In the first case, additional investments occur while the price of production remains constant, regulated by costs on the least fertile land. Since output is increasing, demand must be growing too, to absorb this output at a constant price. Rent increases to the extent that additional output can be produced at lower cost than the price of production. Incidentally, Marx uses the term 'surplus-produce' here in a sense different from that given to it in volume one; here it means the part of output that corresponds to surplus-profit and hence to rent.

Chapter 42. Differential rent II – second case: falling price of production

Increased output may drive down prices and displace land A altogether, so that costs on land B now regulate the price of production. The price fall in itself tends to reduce rents, while the new investments in themselves tend to raise rents. The overall effect could go either way.

Chapter 43. Differential rent II – third case: rising price of production

Marx had not worked out his third case, so Engels did it for him. For the price of production to rise the output of the least productive land must fall, for example as a result of soil exhaustion. (Alternatively, rising demand could bring into use soil that is even less fertile than any that had been used before, a case Engels does not mention.) Falling output because of soil exhaustion lowers rents, while rising price and additional capital investment both raise rents. The net effect, again, is indeterminate.

The chapter concludes with some general comments by Engels and some disconnected fragments from Marx's manuscripts.

Chapter 44. Differential rent also on the worst cultivated soil

If demand is rising and cannot be profitably met at the existing price, the price must rise until additional investments yield average profit. As a result, the worst soil in cultivation may yield rent. Marx provides an example in which the price of production rises from £3 to £3½ to make extra investment on soil B worthwhile. There is a note by Engels, arguing that the new price of production should be regulated by the new *average* cost on soil B. Marx is surely right here and Engels wrong, since it must be profitable to make the *additional* investment. In modern terms, price must cover *marginal* cost.

Engels's confusion is not surprising, since Marx usually argues that price is governed by average, not marginal, cost.

If the additional investment takes place on the worst soil itself, and if it has a still lower yield (higher cost), which is Marx's case (2), then price must rise, as in the case discussed above. Marx seems to contradict himself over whether marginal or average cost (on this particular soil) is the regulator of price of production. If the new investment has a higher yield than the first investment, the (new, lower) average cost must surely regulate price of production (since it is not possible to carry out the second investment and drop the first, so the yield on the first investment is not a relevant margin).

Chapter 45. Absolute ground-rent

In the analysis of differential rent, Marx argues that some part of output yields no surplus-profit (rent), and regulates the price. Rent does not determine prices, it arises only where costs for some part of output are below the cost-determined price, so as to yield surplus-profit. Marx now argues that there is an additional element of rent that does enter into the determination of prices. Here he deviates from Ricardo (but not Smith) in terms of basic principles.

The argument is that landlords will not release any land, even the worst, to farmers unless they get some rent for it. It is not clear what determines the amount of this *absolute rent*. Marx does say that it 'can only be small . . . under normal conditions' (p. 753) because of competition between landlords. If many landlords own parcels of the worst land, each would like to hold back his land to try to get more rent, but each would rather get some rent rather than none at all, so they undercut each other and keep (absolute) rents low. It is not easy to see why Marx wanted to insist on the existence of absolute rent at all.

To cover absolute rent and make cultivation of the worst soil yield average profit, the price of production of grain must rise above the level that would prevail without absolute rent. Marx asks: is this a 'monopoly price'? He defines a monopoly price as a price above value, and argues that the organic composition of capital in agriculture is low, so prices can rise without rising above value. This argument has nothing to do with the cause of absolute rent, only with whether to call the resulting price a 'monopoly price'.

The whole analysis is conducted in terms of the principal agricultural crop. The price of other crops must be set at a level that covers rents determined by the conditions of production of the principal crop. Strictly speaking this is a simplification that is only valid when the principal crop occupies all but a negligibly small part of the land.

Chapter 46. Building site rent. Rent in mining. Price of land

Rent on building sites and on mines is determined in the same way as in agriculture. Wherever a surplus-profit is made because of superior location, because of mineral deposits, or whatever, the landowner can capture the surplus-profit as rent, because the surplus-profit is the result of using a particular piece of land. The principle involved is that which has already been illustrated by the example of water power in chapter thirty-eight.

Monopoly price may cause rent, or vice-versa. Where, say, wine of extraordinary quality can be produced only on some specific pieces of land, its price will rise because of its scarcity (this counts as a monopoly price, in Marx's terminology), yielding a surplus-profit that can be captured as rent. On the other hand, if rents are high on some particular kind of land because it can yield surplus-profit in some other use, the price of products of that land will be correspondingly raised.

Marx finishes the chapter by repeating that the price of land is capitalized rent. It may rise because of a fall in interest rates, because of improvements (which are sold with the land), or because of an increase in rent.

Chapter 47. Genesis of capitalist ground-rent

Section 1. Introductory remarks

In a fully capitalist system, rent is surplus-profit generated in agriculture on top of the general profit rate that accrues to all capitals in agriculture and industry. Rent of this kind obviously did not exist before capitalism, because no general profit rate existed.

Early economists treated rent, not profit, as the normal form of surplus-value, as did the physiocrats (in opposition to the mercantilists, who ignored production altogether and explained surplus-value in terms of circulation). By explaining surplus-value in terms of a surplus output over subsistence requirements, the physiocrats took a step forward. Marx can find no excuse for subsequent writers who explain rent in terms of the physical productiveness of agriculture; physical productivity in the cotton textile industry had increased enormously, after all, but the result was a fall in the value (price) of textiles and not a surplus-profit in that industry. Physical productivity cannot be the explanation of rent in agriculture, when it does not generate corresponding surplus-profits in industry.

Section 2. Labour-rent

Labour-rent was the basis of feudalism and of other pre-capitalist formations. Marx's discussion of it is interesting for the light it throws on his interpretation of history.

Where labour-rent prevails, the direct producers possess means of production and produce their own subsistence, but are compelled by extra-economic means to perform surplus-labour, for example on the lord's estate. In the Asiatic form, the state is the landlord, and rent is extracted in the form of taxes. Labour-rent is a direct and visible form of surplus-labour. Marx adds, in a frequently quoted generalization: 'It is always the direct relationship of the owners of the conditions of production to the direct producers . . . which reveals . . . the hidden basis of the entire social structure, and with it . . . the corresponding specific form of the state' (p. 772).

Labour-rent (like any form of exploitation) is limited by the surplus that can be produced over subsistence. The time spent working for the landlord is generally fixed by custom, since it is in the interests of the 'ruling section of society' to legitimize their exactions by custom and tradition. Development of production may increase productivity, allowing the producers to produce more in the time left to them to work for themselves on their own plots, and thus to acquire a part of the enlarged surplus.

Section 3. Rent in kind

Labour-rent can be transformed into rent in kind, so that the landlord takes the products of surplus-labour rather than taking the labour itself. Rent in kind permits a more rational organization of the producers' time, but does not change anything fundamental. It still presupposes a 'natural' economy in which goods are produced for direct use rather than for sale, though both labour-rent and rent in kind may survive in a commodity producing system.

Section 4. Money-rent

It is even possible for the producer to sell the products of surplus-labour and to hand over the money received, instead of the goods themselves. In money-rent of this kind, the basis of rent is still, as in the previously discussed forms, surplus-labour extracted from peasant producers by extra-economic means. This form of money-rent must not be confused with capitalist ground-rent, which is a surplus-profit over and above the general rate of profit.

Rent as the normal form of surplus-value has reached its final development in money-rent; it evolves either into freehold peasant farming or towards capitalist agriculture and capitalist ground-rent. Once the relation between landowner and producer is a simple contractual tenancy, unsuccessful tenants are soon reduced to propertyless labourers, while those who do well can either buy out the freehold or transform themselves into capitalist farmers.

Section 5. Métayage and peasant proprietorship of land parcels

Métayage (sharecropping) is a transitional form in which landlord and tenant each advance part of the capital required and share the product in agreed proportions.

In a slave economy, or a system in which the owner of a plantation or estate organizes production and pays the labourers, the whole surplus-product accrues to the owner, with no division into profit and rent. In a capitalist context the surplus may be called profit, while in earlier societies it was thought of as rent, but the name by which it is called makes no difference.

Alternatively the peasant may own his land freehold, with no obligation to pay rent, as was the case in classical antiquity (alongside slavery) and again after the decline of feudalism. When capitalism in general is underdeveloped, market prices are not controlled by prices of production, so the elements corresponding to rent and to profit in the peasant's income might be high or low (usually low). The equivalent of differential rent exists, of course; peasants with good land simply do better than those with poor land.

A free, landowning peasantry is a transitional stage, which is undermined by differentiation among the peasantry, by the competition of large scale capitalist farms, by the destruction of rural industry, by the usurpation of common lands, and so on. While it exists, it is a recipe for the progressive impoverishment of the rural population, for inefficiency and for cultural backwardness. It creates 'a class of barbarians standing halfway outside of society' (p. 793). Marx was not given to romanticizing peasant life.

Large scale capitalist agriculture is also inefficient, because it leads to soil exhaustion and to the destruction of human resources through the overexploitation of rural labourers.

PART 7

Revenues and their sources

The third volume of *Capital* is organized around an analysis of the redivision of surplus-value. Marx has shown how surplus-value is converted into profit and redivided between capitals through the equalization of profit rates. Merchant's capital gets its share, in proportion to capital invested. Money is loaned out and becomes money-capital, so profit comes to be divided into interest and profit of enterprise. Landowners take a cut out of surplus-value, as differential and absolute rent, and the general rate of profit is correspondingly reduced.

In everyday life surplus-value in general is quite invisible; all that can be seen are the various forms in which surplus-value is distributed. At the same time, the value of labour-power appears as wages, as the 'price of labour' (already discussed in volume one, part six). According to Marx, economic theories that start from the way things appear in everyday life come up with quite misleading conclusions.

Chapter 48. The trinity formula

At the beginning of the chapter are three fragments garnered by Engels from various parts of Marx's manuscripts. All three cover essentially the same ground, and summarize the message of this whole part of *Capital*.

It seems that capital earns profit, land earns rent, and labour earns wages. There are three 'factors of production', corresponding to three types of revenue. This categorization of revenues and their sources was used by all the economists of Marx's time, and is still found in economics texts today. If profit is divided into interest and profit of enterprise, with the latter regarded as a kind of wage (wages of management), then profit can be eliminated entirely and interest substituted as the revenue of capital.

Marx regards this 'trinity formula' as absurd; capital, land and labour have as much in common as 'lawyer's fees, red beets and music' (p. 794). It is, of course, true that labour, land and means of production (not capital) are essential factors of the labour-process, but the labour-process produces use-values, not exchange-value. Labour creates value, but only in a specific social context. Capital is a social relation, not a thing used in production. Land produces no value, and private ownership of land is a specific, historically determined social relation by which the landowner captures a part of surplus-value.

Marx proceeds to gather together his own analysis, starting with a general overview of the historical role of capitalism. Capitalist production is a transitory, historically determined form of social production. The aggregate of production relations 'is precisely society, considered from the standpoint of its economic structure' (p. 798). Capitalism produces and reproduces the material and social conditions of its existence, and extracts surplus-labour in the form of surplus-value.

Surplus-labour is necessary in any society (socialism included) to provide for the expansion of production. Capitalism is preferable to earlier systems, because it extracts surplus in a way that promotes the development of the forces of production.

The material production process generates a net product, corresponding to $v + s$, which can be consumed (or, in part, accumulated) without exhausting the source of this income. The trinity formula makes capital, labour and land appear as sources of this revenue and of value. It is the ultimate development of fetishism, of the projection of social properties onto material things (land) or the treatment of social relations (labour, capital) as if they were material things.

This fetishized interpretation is made plausible by various features of capitalism that obscure the extraction of surplus-value. The increase in productivity under capitalism appears to be the product of capital itself. Competition redivides surplus-value so that revenues appear to be produced by the factors that enable individuals to capture shares of surplus-value.

Classical political economy destroyed this false appearance by tracing surplus-value to its origins in production, and by showing that average profit was a redivision of the surplus, and rent a surplus over average profit. (Marx must have had Ricardo in mind when he wrote this.) Even the best of the classical economists, however, did not fully shake off the illusion, and the 'vulgar economists' slipped back into superficial appearances. It is, in any case, in the interests of the ruling classes to proclaim the eternal necessity of the categories of income that their position is based on.

Chapter 49. Concerning the analysis of the process of production

Value is produced by labour, and can be divided into necessary and surplus-labour. Marx works over his analysis of the uses of the total product, already dealt with in part three of volume two.

In the last paragraph of the chapter, Marx remarks that, even after the overthrow of capitalism, 'the determination of value continues to prevail in the sense that the regulation of labour-time and the distribution of social labour among the various production groups . . . become more essential than ever' (p. 830). The role of values in a post-capitalist society has been a major subject of debate in the Soviet Union.

Chapter 50. Illusions created by competition

The total (new) value created is divided into wages, profits and rent. These categories of income do not determine the value created; if one of them increases, at least one of the others must fall correspondingly. Marx sets up a number of straw men and knocks them down, to argue that any explanation of income distribution that does not start from values, but works wholly in terms of market-prices and competition, must be incoherent.

Chapter 51. Distribution relations and production relations

John Stuart Mill had argued that production relations were unchanging while the distribution of income could vary from one historical period to another. On the contrary, argues Marx, distribution and production relations are two sides of a coin; capitalist relations of distribution and production are equally transitory. Capital, defined by the production of commodities and the production of surplus-value, reproduces itself as capital and simultaneously generates the various categories of revenue.

Chapter 52. Classes

Capital ends with a fragment of a projected chapter on classes. The three great classes of modern society are wage-labourers, capitalists and landowners. Middle strata of various sorts confuse the issue, but the tendency of capitalist development is to make the dividing lines ever clearer. What is a class? Is it to be identified with a specific source of revenue? The manuscript breaks off without answering the question.

Prefaces and afterwords to *Capital*

Some prefaces are important, some are not. An author may seize the opportunity to explain his intentions and methods, in which case the preface may be an essential introduction to the rest of the work, or he may say, in effect: 'here is a new edition'. Volume one of *Capital* went through two German editions in Marx's lifetime and was also translated into French. After Marx's death, Engels put together volumes two and three from Marx's manuscripts and supervised two further German editions of volume one and a translation into English. Some of the prefaces and afterwords that Marx and Engels produced for these various editions fall into one of the categories described above, some into the other. Only those that contain significant introductory or explanatory comments are discussed below.

Preface to the first German edition

(Written by Marx, dated 1867.) Marx first admits that the opening chapters of *Capital* are difficult (though he claims to have popularized them as far as possible); he urges the reader not to write them off as dealing with minutiae. The value form is basic to the analysis of capitalism, and minutiae matter.

The main part of the preface is aimed at justifying (to a German audience) his extensive use of British examples. England, the most advanced capitalist country, shows what the rest of the world will also become, since the laws of capitalist development work 'with iron necessity toward inevitable results' (p. 8). This is a very strong claim; stronger than Marx usually makes. It is not clear, in the context, which laws he counts as working with 'iron necessity'. Finally, he notes that capitalists are not personally to blame for the evils of capitalism; in his analysis they are no more than the personification of capital.

Afterword to the second German edition

(Marx, 1873) Commenting on the reception of *Capital* in Germany, Marx takes the opportunity to discuss the state of political economy in general. Bourgeois political economy, which accepts capitalist relations of production as natural, can flourish only when class struggle is latent (as in England up to 1830). Once class conflict comes into the open, economists who side with the bourgeoisie become mere apologists. Marx goes on to reply to various criticisms, and to quote (at length) from favourable reviews.

Towards the end of the afterword are some frequently quoted remarks on the dialectical method. Marx distinguishes between the 'method of presentation' and the 'method of inquiry' (see above, p. 13), and distinguishes his method from that of Hegel. To Hegel, the 'idea' was primary, the real world secondary, while for Marx the 'ideal' is no more than the reflection, in men's minds, of the material world. Hegel's dialectic was 'standing on its head'; Marx claims to have turned it right side up, and discovered 'the rational kernel within the mystical shell' (p. 20). This discussion of the dialectic should be read in conjunction with the section on 'The Method of Political Economy' in the introduction to *A Contribution to the Critique of Political Economy* (appendix three, below).

Preface to the English edition

(Engels 1886) After discussing the translation, Engels insists on the need for appropriate technical terms in any science, and in Marxist political economy in particular. He explains Marx's use of quotations to acknowledge the original statement of important ideas, and comments on the situation at the time he was writing, a time of prolonged recession. Finally, he remarks that Marx had thought 'that, at least in Europe, England is the only country where the inevitable social revolution might be effected entirely by peaceful and legal means', though 'he hardly expected the English ruling classes to submit' (p. 6).

Preface to volume two

(Engels, 1885) Engels, as editor, starts with an explanation of how he put the volume together from the manuscripts available to him. He then replies to an accusation that Marx had plagiarized one Rodbertus, by showing that Rodbertus's treatment of surplus-value went no further than that of Adam Smith and of many English socialist writers. Marx's originality, according to Engels, does not lie in his assertion that surplus-value exists, which was already well known, but in the theoretical framework he constructed to explain it, and to do much more. Engels ends with a challenge to Rodbertus's supporters to solve the 'transformation problem' by reconciling the labour theory of value with the formation of a uniform general rate of profit. Marx's solution, in volume three of *Capital*, had not been published at that stage.

Preface to volume three

(Engels, 1894) Marx left the materials for volume three in a very confused state, and Engels begins by discussing the problems that he faced in putting them into publishable form. The remainder of the preface is devoted to a discussion of the responses elicited by Engels's challenge in the preface to volume two (see above). He finds fault with all of the proposed solutions, though an unbiased observer might think that some (Schmidt and Foreman, at least) had covered the essential point, and are ruled out for their non-Marxist language and not for any substantive error.

APPENDIX 2

The Communist Manifesto

The *Communist Manifesto* was written by Marx and Engels in 1847 on behalf of the Communist League. (The final draft was Marx's work.) The prophetic words of the preamble ('A spectre is haunting Europe – the spectre of communism.') were somewhat boastful at the time, since the Communist League had no more than a handful of adherents.

1. Bourgeois and proletarians

The first section of the *Manifesto*, titled 'Bourgeois and Proletarians', is complete in itself. Content apart, it is a literary masterpiece, and it is also the best short statement of Marx's view of capitalism. It is constructed in two antithetical parts. The first looks backward to celebrate the rise of the bourgeoisie and their achievements. The second stresses the evils of capitalism, and argues that the development of capitalism creates a proletariat which will ultimately bring it down.

Marx does not explicitly list the theses of historical materialism, but they unmistakeably inform the panoramic overview of the history of capitalism that he presents. The ascent of the bourgeoisie is depicted in terms of the development of successive forms of production (manufacture, modern industry) linked to corresponding stages in the development of political organization (independent urban republics, absolute monarchy, the modern representative state). Capitalism has transformed the world for the better; it has broken down all fixed hierarchies and ancient prejudices and opened up closed societies. 'The bourgeoisie cannot exist without constantly revolutionizing the instruments of production, and thereby the relations of production, and with them the whole relations of society.'

Feudalism failed, and was swept away, because forces of production were developing inside feudal society that could not be contained within it. Feudal property relations 'had to be burst asunder; they were burst asunder.' Capitalism will suffer the same fate; the inadequacy of capitalist organization is already shown by recurrent commercial crises.

The development of capitalism necessarily entails the development of the proletariat, the class that will overthrow capitalism. The proletariat constantly grows, as the lower strata of the middle class lose their independence and are absorbed into the proletariat. The conditions under which the workers suffer constantly become worse, as modern industry destroys the scope for individual skills and subjects workers to the rhythm of the machine and the despotism of factory discipline. As skills are destroyed, wages fall.

At first the workers were scattered in many small workshops, but they are being gathered into huge factories in the great industrial towns. Trade unions struggle to raise wages and shorten hours of work; their economic gains are constantly reversed, but the real gain is in the growth of working class organization itself. The bourgeoisie, struggling to establish itself, has been forced to recruit the workers as allies, and thus to provide the beginnings of their political education. As polarization proceeds, and as the disintegration of the old society becomes ever more visible, a section of the bourgeoisie goes over to the side of the proletariat, among them a number of intellectuals 'who have raised themselves to the level of comprehending theoretically the historical movement as a whole' (e.g. Marx and Engels).

Previous historical movements were movements of minorities; that of the proletariat is a movement of the overwhelming majority. The proletariat cannot emancipate itself without destroying capitalism root and branch, though it must first 'settle matters' on a national basis. 'What the bourgeoisie . . . produces . . . is its own gravediggers. Its fall and the victory of the proletariat are equally inevitable.'

2. Proletarians and communists

The second section presents the political programme of the communists. It is linked to what has gone before by the claim that communists represent the general interests of the proletariat as they arise from the real historical movement analysed in the previous section.

The basic element in the communist programme is the abolition of private property in its developed form, bourgeois property. It is not a question of depriving peasants and artisans of the hard won fruits of their labour; capitalism has done that already. Capital is a social product and rightfully belongs to society as a whole; the only 'freedom' that communists want to take away is the freedom of the bourgeoisie to subjugate the labour of others.

Communists are accused of wanting to destroy the family, but the bourgeois family is already a mere property relation. They are accused of wanting to abolish nations; the workers have no country. National differences and antagonisms are on the way out anyway, through the development of the world-market. The victory of the proletariat will accelerate this trend, and end the exploitation of one nation by another.

How is all this to be achieved? The first step is the conquest of political power and the establishment of the proletariat (the majority) as the ruling class. The proletariat will then ('by degrees') centralize ownership of means of production in the hands of the state. A list of more immediate demands follows, some of which now seem less than revolutionary, such as a progressive income tax. Once class antagonisms have been abolished, 'the public power will lose its political character', and will cease to be an instrument for the subjugation of one class by another. A society will be established 'in which the free development of each is the condition for the free development of all'.

3. Socialist and communist literature

In 1847 there was little agreement as to what 'socialism' or 'communism' meant, and all sorts of opinions were called 'socialist' simply because they were opposed in some way to capitalism or to the status quo. Marx and Engels therefore found it necessary to categorize and criticize various kinds of 'socialism'.

'Reactionary' socialism in its various forms ('feudal', 'petty bourgeois' and 'German') represents the interests of classes that are threatened by the advance of capitalism, and their desire to recreate the conditions of the past. 'Conservative' or 'bourgeois' socialism represents a futile wish to have capitalism without conflict, a bourgeoisie without a proletariat, which is impossible.

'Critical' or 'utopian' socialism arose at a time when the proletariat was relatively unorganized and unable to take any action on its own behalf. Seeing the workers as victims, not makers, of history, the utopians were led to construct fantastic schemes for the reconstruction of society. As the proletariat develops and rejects these schemes, the utopians turn against the proletariat, and become reactionary.

4. Position of the communists in relation to the various existing opposition parties

Communists support every revolutionary movement, while working to unite all democratic parties and to bring 'the property question' to the front. The *Manifesto* ends with the now famous exhortation: 'The proletariat have nothing to lose but their chains. They have a world to win. WORKING MEN OF ALL COUNTRIES, UNITE.'

Preface and introduction to
A Contribution to the Critique of Political Economy

Preface

After a brief list of the headings under which he planned to publish his work, and a mention of an introduction that he had drafted and omitted (discussed below), Marx states his credentials, in the form of an intellectual autobiography. A short paragraph on his early journalistic career is followed by a long paragraph summarizing 'the guiding principle' of his studies. It is for this paragraph that the preface is justly famous. Brief as it is, it is the best statement of the fundamental ideas of historical materialism. It cannot be adequately paraphrased or summarized, but must be read in full.

First, Marx defines the economic structure of society, the relations of production, which correspond to a certain stage of development of the material forces of production. These are the 'real foundation, on which arises a legal and political superstructure and to which correspond definite forms of social consciousness.'

Second, Marx sets out a process of change. At a certain stage, the material forces of production 'come into conflict with the existing relations of production . . . Then begins an era of social revolution.' The relations of production are transformed and so, eventually, is the whole superstructure. Those who take part in the conflicts of a revolutionary period may not know what they are doing, and such a period should not be judged in terms of the declared aims of the participants.

Society evolves through various stages: Asiatic, ancient, feudal and 'modern bourgeois' (capitalist); the latter is the last 'antagonistic' (class divided) mode of production. The 'prehistory of human society' is about to end.

The remainder of the preface completes the outline of Marx's career and of his studies of economics.

Introduction

The status of the '*Introduction*' is hard to define. It was written in 1857, before the *Grundrisse*. Marx says in the preface that the general introduction that he had drafted was omitted because it anticipated results yet to be established. After the publication of *Capital*, that objection presumably no longer holds, but it remains unclear whether Marx would have altered it had he prepared it for publication. Manuscripts that Marx himself chose not to publish should always be treated with caution.

The manuscript was unearthed and published in 1903, and has since then often been included in editions of the *Contribution*, sometimes titled *Introduction*, sometimes with other titles, such as *Production*, *Consumption*, *Distribution*, *Exchange*. Since the publication of the *Grundrisse* it has also been made available as part of that work.

1. Production

Marx starts by dismissing any method that starts from a hypothetical isolated individual; production is always social. The idea of the self-sufficient individual is itself a product of social development, of the breakdown of simple communities and the rise of commodity production. There are, indeed, some features of production that are common to all societies, and these may validly be set out to avoid unnecessary repetition, but they take very different forms in different societies.

Bourgeois economists who discuss 'production in general' do so to smuggle in categories appropriate to capitalist production and so make them appear to be universal. Property, for example, in the sense of rules governing both access to means of production and distribution of the product, is universal, but private property is not. Provisions to protect property are also universal; the correct conclusion is not that bourgeois law is universal, but that each mode of production generates a corresponding set of legal relations.

2. The general relations of production to distribution, exchange and consumption

Still on the level of 'production in general', Marx launches into a parody of Hegelian logic; the 'unity of opposites' (for example) is exemplified by production and consumption, which are in some sense opposites, but which presuppose each other.

By 'distribution', Marx means the allocation of shares of the product to individuals, while by 'exchange', he means the process by which individuals get the particular things which they consume. For example, in a capitalist system total revenue is paid out as wages, profits, and so on, all in money (distribution), and the recipients then buy particular things with the money (exchange). Consumption includes all using up of produced goods, including 'productive consumption' (use of materials, fuels, etc.). 'Production' is straightforward and needs no definition.

Production and consumption determine each other; things can only be consumed if they have been produced, while production would be pointless if it were not directed to consumption. Consumers' wants shape production, but production also shapes consumers' wants. Distribution and exchange stand between production and consumption.

The form of distribution depends on the organization of production; wages are only paid in a capitalist system which involves wage-labour, and so on. 'The structure of distribution is entirely determined by the structure of production.' Marx discusses conquest, because it appears to be a case in which the mode of production and distribution are imposed from outside, and he argues that the new relations of production and distribution are still the result of the previous modes of production of the conquering and conquered peoples.

Exchange too is governed by production. Exchange of finished consumer goods is governed by the extent of the division of labour, the level of development of production, and so on. Exchange of means of production is directly governed by the structure of production.

Marx concludes that production, distribution, exchange and consumption are interrelated elements of a single whole, and the mode of production is the decisive determinant of the other elements and of the relations between them.

3. The method of political economy

The section on the method of political economy should be read in conjunction with the (even briefer) discussion of method in the afterword to the second German edition of *Capital* (see appendix one, above).

Scientific political economy, Marx argues, must be constructed in two stages, moving first from the concrete to the abstract, then back from the abstract to the concrete. His example is population. Simply to state the number of people in a country is unhelpful. To analyse population further, for example into classes, requires appropriate concepts (working class, hence wage-labour and capital, and so on). The first stage, then, is a movement from the chaotic concrete to construct a set of simple, abstract concepts. This corresponds to the 'method of inquiry' mentioned in the afterword to *Capital*. Given appropriate concepts, the concrete can be reconstructed as 'a totality comprising many determinations and relations'. This is the 'method of presentation'. The concrete is the real starting point, but it appears in the result as a conclusion.

Hegel was misled into thinking the real world was constituted by thought from abstract concepts. On the contrary, abstract concepts are a product of thinking, and the world is quite unaffected by thought until we *act* in reality to change it.

Do simple categories precede more complex forms historically as well as in the theoretical reconstruction of reality? (Hegel thought they did.) Marx answers that in some cases they do and in some they do not. Money, for example, precedes more complex forms, such as industrial capital (the two chapters into which the *Grundrisse* is divided are on 'money' and 'capital') but on the other hand, a complex division of labour is possible without money (as in pre-Columbian Peru). The concept of labour in general, abstract labour, as the source of wealth and of value (see *Capital*, chapter one) was introduced by Adam Smith, and could not have been conceived in its simple, general form until capitalist production had reached a certain stage of development. Real history is more than a dance of abstract concepts.

The order of analysis and of presentation of different concepts cannot be settled in general, without a concrete historical reference. In each society a particular kind or form of production dominates, and determines the place of others. It must be the starting point. In agricultural societies, even the forms of property in manufacture have 'agrarian' features, while in modern bourgeois society, agriculture is a branch of industry, and the analysis of capital must be the point of departure. The order of concepts must be determined by the structure of modern society, and not by their historical order of appearance. (Hence, primitive accumulation is relegated to the end of volume one of *Capital*, after the discussion of fully formed capitalism.)

4. Production

The final section is clearly unfinished. It starts with some notes Marx wrote to himself, listing further points to be discussed, and concludes, somewhat incongruously, with a discussion of Greek art, or rather, of the question: how can Greek art still give pleasure when it was produced for a society so different from that of today?

Glossary

Marx's system of concepts is an integrated whole. His technical terms can, in general, only be defined in terms of that system of concepts and theories, so the glossary entries below can only serve to refresh the memory. For fuller discussion see the relevant parts of *Capital* and the corresponding commentaries in this guide.

Cross-references have been kept to a minimum, since almost all of Marx's terms are ultimately linked to all the others; any attempt at complete cross-referencing would get out of hand. Many of Marx's concepts are subdivisions of more fundamental concepts; they are listed under the main concept, which is often the second word, so, for example, 'constant capital' is listed under 'capital, constant'.

References in brackets are to the volume (v), part (pt), chapter (ch) and section (s) in *Capital* in which the concept concerned is introduced and discussed.

ACCUMULATION
  of capital: *see* reproduction, expanded.
  primitive: historical process by which capital(ism) came into existence (v1, pt8).
BILL OF EXCHANGE: credit instrument widely used in Marx's time; see p. 17 above.
BOURGEOISIE: capitalist class, owners of capital.
CAPITAL: privately owned wealth or value used to generate surplus-value; typical form is industrial capital, but specialized and archaic forms are included by extension; see detailed entries below (v1, pt2, and v1–3, *passim*).
  accumulation of: *see* reproduction, expanded.
  advance of: conversion of money-capital into commodities to generate surplus-value.
  circuit of: circular movement or process by which (industrial) capital produces surplus-value; money-capital is transformed first into productive capital (purchase of labour-power and means of production),

CAPITAL (*cont.*)

next into commodity-capital embodying surplus-value (production), and then into augmented money-capital (realization, i.e. sale of commodities) ready to start again; can be thought of as starting at any of these stages (v1, ch4 and v2, pt1).

circulating: the part of productive capital that is used up in a single cycle of production (v2, ch8).

commercial: *see* capital, merchant's.

commodity-: stage of circuit of capital; commodities embodying surplus-value awaiting sale (v2, ch1, s3).

composition of: measure of ratio of means of production to labour (-power) in productive capital; Marx defines several versions: the *technical composition of capital* is the ratio of the physical mass of means of production to the mass of living labour, and cannot be given a numerical measure; the *value composition of capital* is the ratio of the value of means of production to the value of labour-power employed, hence the ratio of constant to variable capital, c/v; the *organic composition of capital* is the value composition in so far as it reflects changes in the technical composition, i.e. a value weighted index of the technical composition (v1, ch25, s1).

constant: the part of productive capital that consists of means of production (v1, ch8).

fictitious: the capitalized claim to interest payments owned by an individual who has lent money as interest-bearing capital; by extension, other claims to future payments (v3, ch29).

fixed: the part of productive capital which lasts for more than one cycle of production, e.g. buildings, machinery, etc. (v2, ch8).

industrial: capital that produces use-values and surplus-value by going through the entire circuit of capital; all of surplus-value is produced by industrial capital, though some accrues to other claimants (e.g. rent), and some to specialized capitals that perform specialized functions (e.g. merchant's capital); in v1 and v2 industrial capital is often just called 'capital', since other forms are not distinguished until v3.

interest-bearing: money lent in return for interest, typically to industrial capital; the capital is transformed into industrial capital, and the owner is left with fictitious capital (v3, pt5).

merchant's: also called *commercial capital*; specialized fraction of capital which performs functions of buying and selling; pre-dates developed capitalism and may deal in products of non-capitalist producers (v3, pt4).

money-: stage in the circuit of capital; money only counts as money-capital when about to be transformed into productive capital (or commodity-capital, by merchants), except in v3, pt5 where loanable

CAPITAL *(cont.)*

> funds (interest-bearing capital) are referred to as money-capital (v2, ch1, s1).

> *money-dealing*: specialized fraction of capital which performs technical functions such as transfers of money, and gets share of surplus-value (v3, ch19).

> *productive*: a stage in the circuit of capital; divided (a) into variable and constant capital (labour-power and means of production, respectively), and (b) into circulating and fixed capital (used up in one cycle and lasting several cycles of production, respectively); variable capital is all included in circulating capital; constant capital is divided into fixed and circulating constant capital (v2, ch1).

> *turnover of*: process by which particular capital passes through complete circuit of capital; *turnover time of capital* is time taken to pass through complete circuit and can be divided into *time of production* and *time of circulation*; turnover of fixed capital is slower than turnover of circulating capital, so turnover of whole capital is an average (v2, pt2).

> *usurer's*: archaic form of interest-bearing capital; the capital of money-lenders in pre-capitalist societies (v3, ch36).

> *valorization of*: term used in some commentaries for process of producing surplus-value.

> *variable*: part of productive capital; the part of capital advanced to buy labour-power (v1, ch8).

CAPITALISM: mode of production based on relation between capital and wage-labour; Marx does not use the term, but it has come into general use (Marx uses 'capitalist mode of production', 'modern bourgeois mode of production', etc.).

CAPITALIST: owner of capital.

CIRCULATION, SPHERE OF: also called *sphere of exchange*; general term for exchange, i.e. for purchase and sale of commodities, as opposed to production (v1, pt1).

CIVIL SOCIETY: term used by Hegel, and occasionally by Marx; refers to economic and contractual relations between individuals; whole system is divided into state and civil society.

CLASS: set of individuals with common position in production in relation to another class e.g. capitalist class and working class; the precise definition and use of the term is subject to debate.

COMMODITY: thing bought or sold on market (v1, ch1).

> *production*: production for sale; *simple* (also *petty mode of production*), non-capitalist production of commodities by independent producers owning their own means of production.

CONSUMPTION: the using up of use-values, either in *individual consumption* or in *productive consumption* (using up of means of production and labour-power in productive activities).

CO-OPERATION: co-ordinated activity of individuals; form of labour-process in which individuals perform similar tasks without much specialization (precedes manufacture) (v1, ch13).

CREDIT: sale of goods with payment deferred, often by issue of bills of exchange (v3, pt5).

CRISIS: term may be used in general sense (critical situation of any sort); more specifically refers to *periodic crisis*, or stage in industrial cycle in which prices fall, stocks of unsold commodities build up, production and employment are cut, widespread bankruptcies may occur, and financial panic drives interest rates up to exceptionally high levels.

DISCOUNT RATE: interest rate used in discounting bills of exchange, i.e. selling bill before it becomes due, for correspondingly reduced sum of money.

ECONOMICS, POLITICAL ECONOMY: *bourgeois economists* are those who accept capitalism or take it for granted (they need not themselves be members of the bourgeoisie); *classical economics* or *classical political economy* refers to the work of Smith, Ricardo, etc, roughly 1770–1830; *vulgar economics* is Marx's term for the bourgeois economics of the mid-nineteenth century; see pp. 6–11 above.

EXCHANGE, SPHERE OF: *see* circulation, sphere of.

FETISHISM: perception of social relations, social properties, as if they were properties of material things (v1, ch1, s4).

HISTORICAL MATERIALISM: Marx's interpretation of history, see pp. 4–6 above.

HOARD: any quantity of money not in active use; may be held by capitalist, e.g. as reserve-fund, or by others for various reasons.

INDUSTRY
   domestic: production in producer's home; may be for own use, for sale, or under control of capitalist.
   modern: production by machine; succeeds manufacture in development of capitalist labour-process (v1, ch15).

INDUSTRIAL
   cycle: sequence of boom, crisis, slump, recovery; in Marx's time typically with seven to ten year period.
   reserve army: *see* labour, reserve army of.

INTEREST: payment in return for loan, expressed as (percentage) *rate of interest*; rate of interest is determined by demand for and supply of loans; profit can be divided into interest and profit of enterprise; interest rate is normally less than profit rate, except in crises (v3, pt5).

LABOUR: purposive human activity; necessary in any social system to

LABOUR *(cont.)*

produce use-values; in a commodity producing system also produces value (v1–v3, *passim*).

abstract: expenditure of human time and effort in general, regardless of use-value produced; is the substance of value (v1, ch1).

division of: interdependence between producers who carry out complementary tasks; the *social division of labour* involves independent producers of distinct, complete commodities, and is co-ordinated by market forces; the *detail division of labour* or *division of labour in the workshop* involves workers who each carry out a particular specialized stage in the production of a single commodity, and is co-ordinated by a single employer (v1, ch14).

instruments of: tools, equipment, etc. (v1, ch7).

necessary: labour-time required to reproduce value of labour-power; in capitalist system is part of working-day, and remainder is surplus-labour; not to be confused with 'socially necessary labour' (v1, ch9).

-power: the capacity to work, to perform labour; capitalist buys workers' labour-power, extracts actual labour (which is 'the use-value of labour-power') (v1, ch6); *price of*, wages (v1, pt6); *value of, see* value of labour-power.

-process: the production of use-values; labour works on subjects of labour (materials, etc.) using instruments of labour (tools, etc.); subjects and instruments of labour (means of production) derive ultimately from nature (so men transform nature through labour) but are usually products of earlier labour-processes (v1, ch7).

productive: productive labour in general, also called *useful labour*, is labour that produces use-values (v1, ch1, s2); labour is *productive for capital* only if it produces surplus-value; labour expended in commercial activities is not productive in either sense (v1, ch16).

reserve army of: also called *relative surplus-population* or *industrial reserve army*; unemployed or underemployed workers who compete for jobs and keep wages down; constantly replenished by mechanization and by crises; Marx divides it into various parts; the *floating reserve army* consists of currently unemployed industrial workers; the *latent reserve army* consists of underemployed agricultural workers who will move or may move to industrial centres; the *stagnant reserve army* consists of casual or seasonal workers employed irregularly and paid low wages (v1, ch25).

socially necessary: labour-time required to produce a particular commodity under average or normal conditions; determined value (v1, ch1 and v3, ch10).

subjects of: materials worked on and transformed by labour (v1, ch7).

surplus-: labour that enriches an exploiting class and not the labourer; surplus-labour is performed in all class-divided societies; in a capitalist wage-labour system, takes form of surplus-value (v1, ch9).

LABOUR (*cont.*)

    wage-: system in which capitalist buys labour-power and extracts surplus-value; wage-labour implies existence of capital, and vice-versa; unproductive wage-labourers produce no value or surplus-value but perform surplus-labour (v1, ch6–9 and v1–v3, *passim*).

LABOURER: worker; in Marx's usage includes all workers regardless of level of skill.

    collective: set of workers who together produce use-values; includes workers who do not individually produce an identifiable use-value or a distinct commodity, but whose efforts are necessary to the result; in particular, participants in detail division of labour (v1, ch14).

    detail: participant in detail division of labour (v1, ch14).

    wage-: worker in capitalist system of wage-labour (v1, ch6).

LANDED PROPERTY: ownership of land, including mines, fishing grounds, etc.; owner receives rent; in a capitalist system, owner receives 'capitalist ground-rent', which is quite different from earlier forms, such as 'labour-rent' in feudal system (v3, ch37).

MANUFACTURE: production using handicraft methods, but with detail division of labour; follows simple co-operation and precedes modern industry; dominant in England from about 1550 to 1770, and associated with dominance of merchant's capital (v1, ch14).

MERCANTILISTS: economists of sixteenth to eighteenth centuries; see p. 7 above.

MONEY: Marx assumes that a produced commodity (typically gold) serves as money; money therefore has value in its own right; the value of other commodities is expressed in terms of quantities of money (i.e. gold) which serves as *universal equivalent* (v1, ch1, s3); a standard weight of the money commodity may be given a specific name (pound sterling, dollar) and serves as a *standard price* (v1, ch3, s1); goods are exchanged for money, not directly bartered, so money serves as *circulating medium* (v1, ch3, s2), and symbols or substitutes for metallic money (coins, notes) may serve this purpose; money serves as *means of purchase* when exchanged for commodities direct, and as *means of payment* when used to settle debts (v1, ch3, s3); money may also be hoarded; in a developed credit system, various credit instruments may circulate in place of money, and are called *credit money* (v3, ch33).

NATURAL ECONOMY: opposite of commodity production; system of production for direct use and not for sale.

PHYSIOCRATS: school of eighteenth-century French economists; see p. 7 above.

POPULATION: relative surplus population *see* labour, reserve army of.

PRICE: money actually paid for a commodity, not to be confused with value.

PRICE (*cont.*)

    cost-: price or value of means of production and labour-power used to produce a commodity; cost-price is less than value because it does not include surplus-value (v3, ch1).

    of production: price sufficient to yield the average (general) rate of profit on capital advanced; prices tend to prices of production (not values) through equalization of profit rates (v3, pt2).

PRODUCTION

    forces of: extent of human control over nature; general term for level of development of material production.

    means of: material prerequisites of production, apart from living labour; consists of subjects and instruments of labour (v1, ch7).

    mode of: Marx uses this term (a) loosely, to mean the way production is organized and carried out, and (b) more specifically as follows: basic form or stage of economic organization, defined by characteristic form of social relations of production, defining specific classes, and correlated with certain level of forces of production; successive dominant modes characterize different historical periods: (1) *primitive-communal* mode (classless, low level of production); (2) *ancient* mode (Greece, Rome, slavery); (3) *feudalism* (lords exploit serfs through labour-rent); (4) *capitalism* (capital and wage-labour); (5) *future classless* mode ('freely associated producers') not described in detail by Marx; also two modes not in main sequence: (6) *simple commodity production* (independent producers owning own means of production); (7) *Asiatic* mode (communal village producers exploited by tax-rent).

    price of: *see* price.

    social relations of: relationships of ownership and possession of means of production, appropriation of products, hence relations of exploitation; each mode of production has characteristic form of social relations of production; capitalist social relations involve capital and wage-labour.

    sphere of: in commodity producing systems can be distinguished from sphere of circulation (v1, ch6).

PROFIT: that part of surplus-value which accrues to owner of capital (as opposed to ground-rent) (v3, pts 1 and 7).

    of enterprise: the part of profit that accrues to active capitalist after deduction of actual or notional interest (v3, ch23).

    rate of: profit as fraction (or percentage) of capital advanced; competition leads to *equalization of profit rates* and establishment of a uniform *general rate of profit* equal (according to Marx) to the *average rate of profit* which would exist if prices were proportional to values (v3, pts 1–3).

    surplus-: profit above general rate of profit gained by low-cost producers; may be captured by landowners as ground rent (v3, ch10).

PROLETARIAT: working class, class of propertyless wage-labourers.

REALIZATION: stage in circuit of capital and in reproduction of capital; sale of commodities incorporating surplus-value.

RENT: also called *ground-rent*; revenue of owners of landed property; in developed capitalism, ground rent is part of surplus-value (the rest is profit) and is the converted form of surplus-profit in agriculture (and other land-using activities); capitalist ground-rent can be divided into *differential rent*, on all but the least productive land, and *absolute rent*, on all land; capitalist ground-rent must be distinguished from earlier forms; in classic feudalism, all surplus-labour was extracted as rent (not just a part as in capitalism), either as *labour-rent* (unpaid labour on landowner's crops) or as *rent in kind* or *money-rent* (converted forms of labour-rent); in the Asiatic mode, labour-rent was extracted by the state as *tax-rent* (v3, pt6).

REPRODUCTION: preservation of economic and social system by continual reconstitution of material conditions of production (means of production, labour force) and of social relations of production (relations of ownership, class relations); in capitalist system involves *reproduction of capital* (v1, pt7 and v2, pts 1 and 3).

   expanded: also called *extended reproduction*, *accumulation of capital*, *reproduction on an expanded scale*; use of part of surplus-value to add to capital, to purchase additional means of production and labour-power so as to expand the scale of production (v1, pt7, and v2, pts 1 and 3).

   simple: reproduction on an unchanging scale, as opposed to expanded reproduction (v1, ch25, and v2, chs2, 17 and 20).

RESERVE ARMY: *see* labour, reserve army of.

SURPLUS-VALUE: *see* value, surplus-.

TRANSFORMATION PROBLEM: transformation of values into prices of production; Marx's self-imposed task of explaining prices of production in terms of values, and the general rate of profit in terms of surplus-value (v3, pt2).

TURNOVER: *see* capital, turnover of.

VALUE: commodities have *use-value*, the capacity to satisfy wants, and *exchange-value*, the property of being exchangeable for other things; use-value is a precondition for exchange-value, but does not determine its magnitude; the *value* (unqualified) of a commodity is the socially necessary labour-time required to reproduce it; value in this sense underlies and indirectly determines exchange-value (price); in v1 and v2 Marx assumes that prices are proportional to values, a simplification that is corrected in v3, pt2; values are expressed in terms of the value of some other commodity, normally the money commodity, the universal equivalent (v1, pt1).

   absolute surplus-: change in (rate of) surplus-value by increase in working-day (cf. relative surplus-value) (v1, pt3; defined in v1. ch12).

annual rate of surplus-: surplus-value produced per year divided by variable capital advanced; equals rate of surplus-value multiplied by number of turnovers per year (v2, ch16, s1).

exchange-: the property of being exchangeable for other commodities; price is exchange-value expressed in terms of money (v1, pt1).

of labour-power: labour-time socially necessary to reproduce labour-power; equals value of commodities needed to maintain worker's ability to work and to produce successors to present generation (children); contains 'historical and moral element' (vl. ch6).

rate of surplus-: also called *rate of exploitation*; surplus-value per turnover divided by variable capital advanced; equal to *surplus-labour* divided by *necessary labour* or, in the conventional notation, *s/v* (v1, ch9).

relative surplus-: change in (rate of) surplus-value caused by increase in productivity, which reduces value of commodities consumed by workers, hence reduces value of labour-power, hence reduces necessary labour and increases surplus-labour with given length of working-day (v1, ch12).

surplus-: form in which surplus-labour is extracted in capitalist system; source of all capitalist property incomes; possible because value created by (day's) labour exceeds value of (day's) labour-power (v1, pt3).

use-: the property of satisfying needs, either directly, through individual consumption, or indirectly, by producing other use-values through productive consumption; a product may have use-value without being a commodity; all societies produce use-values, but only some produce commodities (v1, ch1).

WAGE: price of labour-power; may be paid as *time-wage* (per unit of time worked) or as *piece-wage* (per unit produced) (v1, pt6).

of management: also called *wage of superintendence*; wage paid to manager, either actual (where manager is employed) or notional (where capitalist acts as manager) (v3, ch23).

Notes

1 (p. 22) The labour theory of value cannot be assessed in isolation, so the debate involves a variety of issues, particularly the 'transformation problem', the question of the relation between values and prices (dealt with by Marx in volume three, part two). The literature is immense, and the references that follow are intended only as possible starting points for further reading.

There are many general works on Marxist economics. Two of them are: Meghnad Desai, *Marxian Economics* (Oxford, Blackwell, 1979), and M.C. Howard and J.E. King, *The Political Economy of Marx* (Harlow, Longman, 1975). A variety of views on labour values are to be found in Ian Steedman *et al.*, *The Value Controversy* (London, NLB, 1981).

There is now general agreement on the correct formal solution of the 'transformation problem', and on the determinants of prices of production. The first correct solution was by L. Bortkiewicz in 1907, and the theory has been refined by subsequent writers. See Desai, or Howard and King. Debate has focussed on two questions.

First, are labour values now superfluous, since prices of production can be derived directly from physical production data and from information about the real wage? See Paul A. Samuelson, 'Understanding the Marxian notion of exploitation: a summary of the so-called transformation problem between Marxian values and competitive prices', *Journal of Economic Literature*, 9, (1971), 399–431, Ian Steedman, *Marx after Sraffa* (London, NLB, 1977), and Anwar Shaikh, 'The poverty of algebra' in Steedman *et al.*, *The Value Controversy*, pp. 266–300.

Second, does the 'fundamental Marxian theorem', showing that surplus-value is a necessary and sufficient condition for positive profits, rescue Marx's analysis, and does it hold for cases involving joint-production? See Michio Morishima, *Marx's Economics* (Cambridge University Press, 1973), Michio Morishima, 'Marx's economics in the light of modern economic theory', *Econometrica*, 42 (1974), 611–32, Ian Steedman, 'Positive profits with negative surplus value', *Economic*

Journal, 85 (1975), 114–23, Michio Morishima, 'Positive profits with negative surplus value – a comment', *Economic Journal*, 86 (1976), 599–603, with Steedman's reply, *ibid*, 604–8, Elmar Wolfstetter, 'Positive profits with negative surplus value: a comment', *Economic Journal*, 86 (1976), 864–72, with Steedman's reply, *ibid*, 873–6, and Steedman, *Marx after Sraffa*.

A somewhat different approach is to start by defining a measure of 'exploitation', and to proceed from there to examine the concept of value. See John E. Roemer, *A General Theory of Exploitation and Class* (Cambridge, Mass., Harvard University Press, 1982), and Heinz Holländer, 'Class antagonism, exploitation and the labour theory of value', *Economic Journal*, 92 (1981), 868–85.

Many of the works cited above make substantial use of mathematics, and so they should, since the quantitative aspects of values and prices are essentially mathematical. If all else fails, Marx's approach might be defended on the grounds that it, at least, is comprehensible to non-mathematicians.

2 (p. 23) All quotations in the main body of this guide are from *Capital*, and are taken from the section under discussion unless otherwise stated. Page references are to the relevant volume of the edition issued by the Foreign Languages Publishing House, Moscow (Volume I, 1961; Volume II, 1957; Volume III, 1962).

3 (p. 24) For a discussion and bibliography on the issue of heterogeneous labour see Samuel Bowles and Herbert Gintis, 'The Marxian theory of value and heterogeneous labour: a critique and reformulation', *Cambridge Journal of Economics*, 1 (1977), 173–92, and Michio Morishima, 'S. Bowles and H. Gintis on the Marxian theory of value and heterogeneous labour', *Cambridge Journal of Economics*, 2 (1978), 305–10, with a reply by Bowles and Gintis, *ibid*, 311–14.

4 (p. 26) The relation between the logical sequence of development of Marx's theory and the historical development of actual societies has been much discussed, particularly in relation to the 'historical transformation problem', i.e. the question whether there was a historical epoch preceding the full development of capitalism, in which prices tended to values. Marx himself commented, on the general issue, in the introduction to *A Contribution to the Critique of Political Economy*, see appendix three to this guide, pp. 194–5. For a taste of modern discussions see: Ronald Meek, 'Karl Marx's economic method' in R. Meek, *Economics and Ideology and other Essays* (London, Chapman and Hall, 1967); M. Morishima and G. Cataphores, 'Is there an "historical transformation problem"?', *Economic Journal*, 85 (1975), 309–28; and R. Meek, M. Morishima and G. Cataphores, 'Is there an "historical transformation problem"?: an interchange', *Economic Journal*, 86 (1976), 342–52.

5 (p. 66) See Arghiri Emmanuel, *Unequal Exchange, A Study of the Imperialism of Trade* (London, NLB, 1972), and Anthony Brewer, *Marxist Theories of Imperialism, A Critical Survey* (London, RKP, 1980), chapter 9.
6 (p. 139) See n. 1 above.
7 (p. 140) See n. 4 above.
8 (p. 145) See G. Hodgson, 'The falling rate of profit', *New Left Review*, 84 (1974), John E. Roemer, 'Continuing controversy on the falling rate of profit: fixed capital and other issues', *Cambridge Journal of Economics*, 3 (1979), 379–98, and the works by Desai and by Howard and King cited in n. 1 above.

Index